# UNWELCOME
## INHERITANCE

"Lisa Sue Woititz has written a spiritually insightful and timely book, building on her mother's best-selling *Adult Children of Alcoholics*. It clearly examines what Janet Woititz meant when she said, 'I took my energy back and I took my power back. And I put that energy and power into the things that were important to me.' It's a must-read for anyone seeking to heal broken family relationships."

—Father Leo Booth, author of *The Happy Heretic: Seven Spiritual Insights for Healing Religious Codependency*

"If you are someone who had parents (or loved ones) with substance abuse, Lisa's voice allows you to accept this pain in ways that promote taking charge. She shows you how you can move forward. If you're like me, a father of two teenage daughters who had parents and grandparents who suffered from substance abuse, or are someone who can relate to such a circumstance, I recommend you welcome *Unwelcome Inheritance* into your life."

—Fredrick Hahn, author of *Strong Kids, Healthy Kids* and coauthor of *The Slow Burn Fitness Revolution*

"As humans, we have the unique capacity to learn from our history. In *Unwelcome Inheritance*, Lisa Woititz teaches us how to exercise this ability to deepen our recovery and help our families to heal as well. This book is a spiritual lesson that will help shift your thinking from addiction to recovery."

—Rabbi Abraham J. Twerski, M.D., author of *Addictive Thinking*

# UNWELCOME
## INHERITANCE

*Break Your Family's Cycle
of Addictive Behaviors*

**LISA SUE WOITITZ** *and*
**JANET GERINGER WOITITZ, Ed.D.** (1938–1994)

Hazelden
Publishing

Hazelden Publishing
Center City, Minnesota 55012
hazelden.org/bookstore

Library of Congress Cataloging-in-Publication Data

Woititz, Lisa Sue, 1965-
Unwelcome inheritance : break your family's cycle of addictive
    behaviors / Lisa Sue Woititz and Janet Geringer Woititz.
      pages cm
    Includes bibliographical references.
    ISBN 978-1-61649-590-9 (softcover) — ISBN 978-1-61649-594-7 (e-book)
    1. Children of alcoholics. 2. Children of drug abusers. 3. Alcoholism—
      Treatment. 4. Drug abuse—Treatment. 5. Alcoholics—Rehabilitation.
        6. Drug abusers—Rehabilitation. I. Woititz, Janet Geringer. II. Title.
    HV5132.W645 2015
    613.8—dc23

                                                                    2015009814

*Editor's note*
Some names, details, and circumstances have been changed to protect the
privacy of those mentioned in this publication.

   This publication is not intended as a substitute for the advice of health care
professionals.

   Alcoholics Anonymous, AA, and the Big Book are registered trademarks
of Alcoholics Anonymous World Services, Inc.

Janet G. Woititz, list of characteristics of Adult Children of Alcoholics from
*Adult Children of Alcoholics.* Copyright © 1983 by Janet G. Woititz. Reprinted
with the permission of The Permissions Company, Inc., on behalf of Health
Communications, Inc., www.hcibooks.com.

19  18  17            2  3  4  5  6

*Cover design: Percolator*
*Interior design: Terri Kinne*
*Typesetting: Bookmobile Design & Digital Publisher Services*

*In memory of*
   *Robbie, Stacie, and Brad*
   *and*
   *Bill and Lois W.*

## Dedication

*To Dad for his power of example;*
*Rebecca, Michael, and Joshua for their inspiration;*
*Dave for his unconditional love;*
*Danny for his inner strength*

*And to ACoAs and others from all walks of life*
*who identify with this journey*

*With love and gratitude, I dedicate this work to you.*

# Contents

# Acknowledgments

Few people in their lifetime are as blessed as my mother was to have Professor V. Gioia Kay for her best friend, confidante, business partner, and advisor. Fewer people have been as blessed as I am to have her for my godmother and life teacher. I could not love her or appreciate her more, even if she had given birth to me. She has been part of our family and has been with us for every moment of joy or sadness in almost forty years. Most people do not realize that Gioia founded the ACoA movement right along with Mom and was with her every single step of the way until the day Mom passed—just as she has been here with me, envisioning this book and helping to bring it into reality. Boundless love and gratitude for you and the vibrant, brilliant, loving person that you are.

Much gratitude to my brother, Dave Woititz, for keeping Mom's work alive by creating www.drjan.com and for providing such meaningful content for this book. In sharing about my life, I am also sharing about yours, and you are so humble to encourage me to do so.

Loving thankfulness to Ivan Whittenburg for cheering me on every day, for keeping me focused, and for rolling up your sleeves to help me through the most difficult things.

Thanks to my treasured friends: Marilyn Tipp, Lynn Tobin, Alice Bruhns, Christina Breda, Helena Blumer, and Nancy Harrington. You make me feel anything is possible.

It still amazes me every day how George Adams insisted I write a book without ever knowing it was my dream to do so, and without knowing a thing about my family. I can't thank him enough for introducing me to his brilliant and talented daughter, Helen Zimmermann, who became my agent and guided me through the crafting of the only proposal that would have brought Hazelden into my life. Many thanks to Sid Farrar, who saw my vision with more clarity than I did, and who gave me the opportunity to share that vision through this book. Assigning me to work with the masterful Cynthia Orange was a gift that words cannot describe. Cynthia, with your gentle grace and expertise, you brought the writer in me to life, and for that I will always be grateful.

Many thanks to Tim Healy, CASAC and Senior Addiction Counselor at St. John's, for so willingly sharing his expertise and for answering my endless questions with such thoughtfulness and depth. I have the utmost respect for you as a clinician and a friend.

At least three "gratitudes" go to Alice Kroll, NCC, LPC, for teaching me how to live in today and for helping me become the person I was meant to be.

And, thank you to my sweet children, Rebecca, Michael, and Joshua, for your willingness to be included in our story and for your encouragement. I love being your mom.

* * *

# Prologue

It's the end of another chaotic day of my own making. The sun has gone down, and I'm still at my desk, feeling whooped, wishing for an escape from the dread that closes in on me as the day fades away. At fifty, isn't life supposed to be getting easier instead of harder? Instead, here I am cleaning up the emotional and financial wreckage in the wake of a second divorce, with no light at the end of the tunnel anytime soon. When I scold myself for creating all of these problems, I can hear Mom respond, "But you came by it all honestly. You were set up for your troubles."

In other words, she's telling me that many of my adult problems are the result of growing up in a home with alcoholism. It would be great if knowing that truth fixed everything, but it doesn't. It's going to take a ton of work—work on the inside and on the outside. Tired and full of self-pity and fear, I want to escape my feelings. I could zip around the corner and pick up a pint of ice cream, but I tell myself *no*. I wish that I could smoke a few hits of pot, and at the same time I am glad that I don't have any. (If I did, I'd have to smoke it all.) If I liked bars, I'd go out and order two Washington Apples with Crown Royal whiskey instead of vodka—just enough to take the edge off, but not enough to knock me on my ass. Pills aren't my thing either, although I did give them a fair try (by prescription, of course). Antidepressants make me feel suicidal, antianxiety meds make me feel insane, and sleeping pills keep me awake—the classic paradoxical response that my mother believed children of alcoholics often have to medications. So here I just sit, immobilized and alone with my thoughts, my brain like a tennis ball being lobbed back and forth between fear and faith—between "It will be all right" and "OMG, I'm gonna die."

Forty years of personal and professional education about alcoholism and its effects on those closest to the alcoholic have done so little to stop this disease from continuing to sink its claws into my family. The fact that my mother wrote the book that helped launch today's Adult Children of Alcoholics (ACoA) movement did not exempt me or my two brothers from the impact of growing up in a violent alcoholic household, nor did it stop me from re-creating the chaos of my childhood in my own household despite my solemn vows to the contrary. My little brother was born just a few months before my father got sober, so he doesn't remember alcoholism in our home, but, as ACoAs know all too well, he also lived with the consequences of having an addicted parent. My older brother shared the trauma I recount in this book, but I feel that his is not my story to tell. So the childhood experiences I relate are those seen through my eyes and from my perspective. However, I am happy to report that, thanks to what Mom taught us and so many others about what it means to be an ACoA, my siblings and I enjoy a healthy and close relationship today.

How ironic that, while Mom traveled the world helping ACoAs heal from their childhoods, she could not help me because one cannot be a therapist to her own child. Likewise, the fact that my father will soon celebrate forty years of sobriety and is considered an "old-timer" in recovery had deluded me into believing that I was somehow immune from the disease of addiction.

It took me decades to admit that intellectual knowledge is not healing, and it took many extra years for me to seek help because of the arrogance that can come with being the child of a celebrity. For so long, the self-destructive influences of the past seemed stronger than my ability to thwart them with self-respect and love. Now I can accept that the disease of addiction lives in my cells—a demon that waits patiently for my attention. With this reality always in mind, I renew my commitment to live in recovery on a daily basis, knowing that breaking the cycle of addictive behavior in my family begins with me.

* * *

# Introduction

We refer to them as Adult Children because though they are
chronologically adults, because of the environment they were
brought up in and the fact that they have really had to bring
themselves up, in some areas of their lives their maturity level
is more like that of a child than an adult. So there is an adult
that became an adult too soon in some ways, and a child that
didn't have the parenting that they may have needed in order
to develop in other ways.[1] —Dr. Jan

My name is Lisa, and I am an adult child of an alcoholic—an
"ACoA," to use the popular acronym. My late mother, Dr. Janet
Geringer Woititz, who wrote the definitive book on the subject titled *Adult Children of Alcoholics,* liked to refer to me as
the "first" ACoA because, she said, her theories about this phenomenon were sparked by observing my behaviors as a child
struggling to "grow up" in a home with an alcoholic father.

Mom was not the child of an alcoholic. She was, however,
married to my father, who was an alcoholic, and as his disease
progressed, the violence in our home escalated, and the isolation and powerlessness we all felt intensified. She could see
what was happening to my two brothers and me and realized
that what went on in our house was different than what was

going on in other houses. Although she was suffering right along with us, she intuitively knew that the hell we were living in would impact the rest of our lives. She tried in vain to get help. As she put it,

> I couldn't get anyone to listen. They said, "Well, if your alcoholic gets well, then you get well, and if you get well, the kids will get well." It doesn't seem right to me. That can't be the way it has to be. What happens to my kids cannot be contingent on me and cannot be contingent on their father. There's something else going on here. So what you see are the results, or at least my part of it are the results of a mother screaming very largely on behalf of her own three very wonderful, special, healthy children.[2] —Dr. Jan

Mom's work in this field was born out of her burning desire to bring attention to this problem so she could help other families like ours. She went to night classes at Montclair State College to earn her master's degree in counseling, after which she established her private practice. Early on, she saw clients in the family room of our house, but my dad made it very hard for her to work. There were a lot of episodes where he would barge into her sessions with clients, including one session with a client who was experiencing an LSD flashback.

Finally empowered enough to leave an unhealthy marriage, Mom divorced my dad when I was going into high school. She continued her education, working on her doctoral thesis about the children of alcoholics and how they carried the impact of their childhood experiences into adulthood. She believed that they could grow up with issues stemming from childhood that would really get in the way of being happy, productive, successful adults with healthy intimate relationships. She tells a funny story about her experience of working on that thesis, which eventually evolved into the best seller *Adult Children of Alcoholics*:

I was invited to speak about ACoAs at a Recovery Fest in Minneapolis. About ten thousand people attended. Ten years before they couldn't have had a Recovery Fest for ACoAs. There was no ACoA "recovery" then because people would not own up to the fact that there was a problem even though a couple of us were going around saying, "There is something terribly wrong." I did my dissertation on children of alcoholics, and I was told at that time that what I was doing was irrelevant and insignificant and I would never be proud of it. That was the one thing that my committee agreed on [laughter on the tape from Dr. Jan and the audience].

I was living with an active alcoholic, and as those of you who have lived with alcoholism know, that's the way we often talk to each other, so I didn't realize they were discouraging me! And I went ahead with the project.[3] —*Dr. Jan*

When others who were bruised by the effects of alcoholism in their families began meeting in our home, I couldn't stop myself from eavesdropping on their fascinating, sometimes jaw-dropping conversations. As they shared their personal experiences, they came up with a list of characteristics that adult children of alcoholics had in common, and I soon realized that they were describing *me* in the future. They were talking about *my* home and family. I watched through the eyes of a child as a grassroots movement began in 1981 with that small group and then exploded into an industry when Mom's books *Adult Children of Alcoholics* and *Struggle for Intimacy* made their way onto the *New York Times* Best Sellers list almost exclusively by word of mouth.

Sadly, Mom—who was affectionately known as "Dr. Jan"— passed away in 1994 at the young age of fifty-five. Many even call her the "mother of ACoA" because her book *Adult Children of Alcoholics* opened a pathway to healing for millions of people around the world who, before her, could not even put a name to their problem. Although the Twelve Step ACA groups in existence today are not the ones Mom started, the gift of her insight and intuition, coupled with an uncanny ability to connect deeply and immediately to anyone, was the catalyst of a movement that would literally change the world for generations to come.

As a preteen, I assisted Mom in her research about children of alcoholics, which validated what she already knew about me. I distributed surveys and helped organize the data. While in high school, I transcribed her notes into manuscripts. In my college days, I helped to organize focus groups at her clinic, the Institute for Counseling and Training, where we served ACoAs and others affected by alcoholism and other addictive disorders. I was in my senior year of college on my way to class when I got the call with the amazing news about Mom's book *Adult Children of Alcoholics* becoming a best seller. We jumped for joy and celebrated our success as a family helping other families, and we watched in awe as it remained on the *New York Times* list for almost a year. For much of that time, *Struggle for Intimacy* was also on the list. This success meant that our family secret was one shared by many other families, and there was great relief in the reality that we were all journeying together.

I'm grateful that Mom gave a name and a voice to what my brothers and I had grown up with—and in doing so, that she was able to help others around the world and from all walks of life by giving them a place to begin healing. Yet I remember feeling jealous of all of those people who had more time with her than I did. I remember thinking how ironic it was that they all got so much help, and I never got the help I needed. While Mom traveled, lecturing and teaching and appearing on radio and television, I was left unsupervised, and—as the following pages will reveal—I got into a heck of a lot of trouble!

After college, I became program director at the clinic, where I designed and implemented educational programs and support groups for ACoAs and created and supervised a summer camp for our adult clients who had never had this experience as children. I handled media requests and eventually began to supervise daily operations and staff as my mother's illness took her health and eventually her life.

This has been my lens on the world since I was a young child. This has been my life. More than twenty years after she passed away, Dr. Jan's work continues to serve as the foundation for healing for the continuing generations of ACoAs as the number of people affected by the disease of alcoholism—either in themselves or their loved ones—continues to grow. Her work is required reading in many college and substance abuse courses. (A complete list of her books can be found in About the Authors at the end of this book.) Book sales number in the millions and remain steady with no promotion and advertising, illuminating the fact that the need for help is still out there and isn't going away.

As time marched on, it became clear that adult children of alcoholics were not the only people seeking out Dr. Jan's books. People of all ages from all sorts of troubled backgrounds related to the characteristics that ACoAs share in common. As Dr. Jan often said, "The adult child of an alcoholic knows no age. It doesn't matter whether they are five or fifty-five."

Dr. Jan's final work, *Healthy Parenting,* was written with the goal of bringing to light the unique struggles that we adult children of alcoholics encounter as parents, and how our upbringing impacts our children. How can we raise healthy children when we have no frame of reference for what that means? Sadly, by the time this important book was published, Mom was so ill that she could not promote it in a meaningful way.

*Unwelcome Inheritance* is the next logical step in helping ACoAs continue their healing process into the next generation. It describes how we accomplish this by taking our understanding of our past experiences to the next level and also by taking a deeper look at how we live our lives today. It discusses how the impact of alcoholism on our children is every bit as lasting as the way our parents' alcoholism and other addictions affected us and how repairing our broken relationships with our parents and other family members can help break the cycle of addiction with our children. As I discovered, my healing from growing up with alcoholism was not as complete as I thought it was, and in some aspects I'm still reacting to the past in my daily life and as a parent.

*Unwelcome Inheritance* brings together my knowledge and experience and Dr. Jan's previous and unpublished work on this subject to further educate my fellow ACoAs, whose children have addiction problems despite our best efforts to break the cycle. So many of us have tried it all: teaching our children about the disease of addiction, sharing about our painful childhood experiences, and even exposing our own addictions in an effort to ward off the inevitable. We try to be the best parents we know how to be, yet alcoholism does not always respect our boundaries. As one ACoA said, "We see it [our kids' substance abuse] coming like a runaway train but feel powerless to stop it."

Perhaps many of us unknowingly enabled our children in their substance abuse because of our own upbringing, or we've modeled our own addictive behaviors without meaning to. In these pages, I hope to bring these dynamics to light so that we can take a clear look at how we got here and what we can (or can't do) to help our children and ourselves. In the end, we just might discover what we hope our kids have always known: that we are better parents than we realize and that our kids know how much we love them.

If you, like so many of us ACoAs, have seen yourself through the eyes of a victim throughout your entire life, then letting go of this view of the world is scary. But it will be okay! Feelings are not facts. Identifying with other ACoAs has helped me see myself as part of a chain instead of a lonely dot in the universe and within the context of a larger story that has fascinated and empowered me. *Unwelcome Inheritance* is designed to inspire readers to live the well-known and beloved anonymous prayer that hung on the wall in the kitchen of my childhood home:

> *God, grant me the serenity*
> *to accept the things I cannot change,*
> *courage to change the things I can,*
> *and wisdom to know the difference.*

Think of this book as a conversation among me, Dr. Jan, ACoAs, and others who share our experiences. Welcome to this new discussion, with a look at how we got here and what we can do to help heal our families, our kids, and ourselves. I hope that you will learn, as I have, that we are pretty damn great just the way we are and that we have done our very best with what our parents taught us.

Every child of an alcoholic or drug addict has a unique story to tell, yet we are alike in so many ways. In chapter 1, "A Childhood from Hell," I share some of my story about growing up in the shadow of alcoholism and an alcoholic father. As you read about my experience, I invite you to reflect on your own story and think about the ways addiction has affected and shaped your life.

Chapter 2, "Unwelcome Inheritance," talks about how alcoholism and addiction can affect our minds, our bodies, and our spirits. It also describes the characteristics of adult children of alcoholics, discusses what it means to be codependent, and explores how addictive behavior is part of our unwelcome inheritance.

Chapter 3, "A Look at Three Generations," suggests that we ACoAs expand our life view to include the other generations of our families. Doing this helps us to see ourselves as part of history, which takes us out of and beyond ourselves. I offer an example from my own family and include stories from others whose recovery has been enhanced by opening their minds in this way.

The way we are raised dramatically affects the way we raise our children. Chapter 4, "Adult Children as Parents," explores how our upbringing in an alcoholic home can affect us as parents and brings to light many things that ACoA parents have in common. If our children abuse substances, another layer is added to this already challenging and complicated task of parenting, and chapter 5, "Adult Children Raising Alcoholics," is entirely dedicated to this subject.

Ultimately, our goal is to do whatever we can to break the cycle of addiction and addictive behavior that has already been perpetuated throughout the generations of our families, and chapter 6, "Breaking the Cycle," is a realistic discussion about what is within our ability to change and how this change begins with us. We have the power within us to create the family we have always wanted, if we are willing to accept the fact that even those who have hurt us in the past have a story—just like we do.

In chapter 7, "Breaking the Cycle of Anger and Resentment," the story of a friend and her daughter's painful relationship highlights how anger and blame can devastate families and separate them in a permanent way. In contrast, I share my personal transition from anger and blame to acceptance and healing as a testament that it is possible to break this cycle.

The final chapter, "Changing the Things We Can," asks readers to try to step into the shoes of the estranged people in their lives, if they can. If it is possible to do this, we might be able to see the world through their eyes and hopefully come to understand the story that brought that other person to where they are today. Reconciling our broken family relationships can be a giant step toward breaking the cycle of our unwelcome inheritance, and it is the goal or dream for many—perhaps most—ACoAs. But, as this chapter acknowledges, this goal might not be achievable (or advisable) for ACoAs for whom reconnecting with family might be dangerous or unhealthy. In these cases, ACoAs may choose to create a new family where they can be safe and thrive.

Throughout *Unwelcome Inheritance,* Dr. Jan's thoughts and advice are shared mostly through her previously unpublished writings. In addition, each chapter ends with a "Takeaway"—a question or tip and a quote from Dr. Jan that links to the issues discussed in the chapter or takes these topics a little deeper.

• • •

CHAPTER 1

# A Childhood from Hell

Inherent in this model of looking at the family is also a model
for looking at children of alcoholics. Because for every generation that has passed along alcoholism, there must be children
affected as well who live out those issues if not treated. And
since so many of these children become alcoholic themselves
(in part because of their physical vulnerabilities and the behavior they learn from their parents), we need to break this
cycle.[1] —Dr. Jan

I remember when I was four years old eavesdropping on my
parents fighting downstairs when I was supposed to be sleeping. As I crouched in a ball outside my bedroom door, I could
hear my drunken father's booming voice vibrate through the
walls below. "God daaaaaamn it!" he bellowed. His bellowing
was followed by my mother's pleading voice, glass smashing,
and her sobbing. I wish I could say this was an unusual occur-
rence, but it was not. It was a scene that played out over and
over again all through my childhood.

Some nights I'd hear the police come to the door. On a few
occasions, I'd wake up in the morning and Mom wouldn't be
there because she had been whisked away to the hospital during
the night. Dad would mumble something about a car accident,

which made no sense, because if that had happened, shouldn't we be with her? During their fights, I'd sit frozen, yet unable to tear myself away. If I heard my father's loud footsteps nearing the stairs, I'd jump into my bed and feign sleep. Then the bedroom door would slam across the hall and the house would become still. My mother would remain downstairs to sleep on the pullout sofa that she bought with the money she made seeing clients. On these occasions, the butterflies in my stomach fluttered madly, keeping me awake until the wee hours when I couldn't fight sleep any longer.

My childhood memories are filed away in my mind according to my grade in school, and each one of those years is represented by a story that springs to mind when that file is opened. Looking back now as a woman with children of my own, with all of these years in between, it is clear that all of those stories have a common thread: a powerless, desperate young child being raised in a family and in a home that was ravaged by alcoholism. I step into the feelings of the young child I am describing and realize that it is *still* me, that the lens through which I view the world is still distorted by my experiences.

On school-day mornings, my mother brought me through the giant red door of the Little Red School House on Park Street and left me there to have a few hours of carefree fun with some delightful children. Mrs. Gannon was my rather scary, stern-faced nursery-school teacher. Did she know that at four years old I was not a spontaneous and naïve little girl anymore? Mom would leave me to fend for myself. I'd hang up my coat in the assigned cubby with the anticipation of a businessman entering his Wall Street office at dawn and disposing of his overcoat before beginning a dramatic day that would end in either dismal failure or huge success. I was a little girl whose mission it was to win the approval of this intimidating teacher, and my efforts seemed to backfire every time.

My little classmates were awed that I was a fluent reader, and in my desperation to be liked, I read *Curious George* to anyone who asked. Mrs. Gannon would usually snap the book from my hands without saying a word but with a look that clearly told me, "Stop that, you show-off!" I remember one time we were at our cubbies getting dressed to play outside in the snow, and I tried to help Billy get his boots on because he looked like he was going to cry. Mrs. Gannon gritted her teeth and told me, "Stop helping him. He has to do it himself!" I felt so ashamed and insecure, wondering—yet again—why she didn't like me. Even at that young age, I recall those feelings as being very familiar: I had often felt them at home. Imagine—four years old and already codependent!

The following year, I began elementary school. After yet another sleepless night, I'd walk to my new sanctuary, Northeast Elementary School. School was a relief from the stress and fear of being home. By first grade, however, my sense of self-worth was already shot, especially in terms of how I expected to be treated by boys. We sat in groups of three in our classroom, and my first crush, David, sat between Suzanne and me. Even though we were inches away from one another, David didn't even know I was alive. He and our classmate Steven both had a mad crush on Julie, and they would vie for her affection by bringing her gifts, trying to outdo one another. I still feel pathetic admitting this, but in my desperation to get David to notice me, I'd bring him gifts to give to Julie. A shrink might hear me describe my school experiences in nursery school and first grade and conclude this was the same desperation I felt when vying for my father's attention. I know now that this behavior was a sign of things to come.

In second grade, I had the prettiest teacher in the whole school, Mrs. Evans. I was her star student. The work was easy, and I was so far ahead of the class that Mrs. Evans had me help her correct my classmates' workbooks while the other kids finished the work I'd completed long before. At conferences, teachers told my mother how they wished they could have thirty of me in their class. How proud she was to repeat that comment to friends and relatives, and for that brief moment, I felt special. But usually I just felt awkward and ashamed—and lonely. The other girls all seemed like such great friends with one another. They all giggled together about their gymnastics class and Hebrew school. I wondered how it was that they got to do these things. I would have adored gymnastics and going to Hebrew school with other Jewish kids. They were so lucky!

I had only one friend at school, Suzy, who had achieved the popularity that I and most kids aspire to. To my surprise, she invited me over to her house a few times. It never occurred to me that one day I would have to reciprocate, and when that day came, it wasn't pretty. When we got to the house, Dad was uncharacteristically home instead of at work and was passed out on the living-room floor when we arrived. My mother nonchalantly explained to Suzy, "Oh, he sleeps on the floor because he has a problem with his back. The doctor told him that sleeping on the floor would help." When I went to a recovery group for teenage children of alcoholics a couple of years later, I learned that my mother's lies were typical behavior in an alcoholic home. Long story short: I never had to worry about what would happen the next time Suzy came over because she never came back. Our friendship was over.

We lived on a pretty tree-lined street in the suburbs of Manhattan, a commuter's paradise. My father was an award-winning broadcast journalist and producer at a major television network. He may have been a high-level executive, but in my view, he was still a "low-bottom" alcoholic, even though he put on that fancy suit and shiny shoes every day and commuted into Manhattan. Our neighborhood was teeming with kids, and we'd often play kickball in the street. My troubles were forgotten during these playtimes until Dad came staggering down the street from the New York City bus stop around the corner, sometimes drunk and bloodied from a fall or two he'd taken somewhere on the way home. Dozens of kids scattered when they saw him coming, just like cockroaches do when the lights go on. I wished then that I could just disappear.

Some afternoons or on a weekend, I'd walk a full mile to Kyle's Drug Store to steal candy. After such petty thefts, I'd go home, hide in my bedroom closet, and enjoy the relief I felt as I gorged myself into a sugar stupor. Even as a little girl, I was like a true addict, taking risks to get ahold of something that might numb my feelings. Like so many children of alcoholics, sugar became my "drug of choice" at an early age.

Sometimes I'd rifle through Mom's coat pockets for change and walk around the corner for ice cream. I'd be gone for at least an hour, but no one seemed to miss me. One day, the pharmacist at Kyle's saw me shove a pound bag of Swedish Fish candy down my pants and walk out of the store. He called Mom, and when I got home, she cried and cried. She was so tired all of the time because of the late-night brawls, and crying made the dark circles under her eyes look even darker and puffier. I don't know whether she was upset because her seven-year-old daughter was caught shoplifting or because she'd never even noticed that I was gone. Was she in denial about her child acting out this way to get the attention she craved? Anyway, I wasn't punished, and the incident was never mentioned again.

Eventually it would be dinnertime, and if Dad weren't already out drinking, we'd usually sit down to eat as a family. One false move, and the meal would end with him blowing his top and slamming the front door on his way out to the bar. I'd be in my pajamas and in bed by the time he returned, and the story would begin again, with me eavesdropping while my parents fought when I was supposed to be in bed sleeping.

By the time I was in third grade, my problems at home began to leak into the classroom in an alarming way. My teacher, Mrs. Gill, was a sweet and warm person who created a relaxed environment where I began to let my guard down. Sometimes she even took us bird watching before school. And she somehow managed to obtain a life-sized motorized camel that had been used in a Macy's display, which was the centerpiece of the classroom. It was majestic, covered with "jewels," and during the Pledge of Allegiance, she turned it on so that the head moved up and down.

Mrs. Gill also acquired a big square metal frame on wheels that we used as our "television set," and each morning we would use it to report the news. The "Newscaster of the Week" would go around the room with a clipboard to see who had a news item to share with the class. I signed up almost every morning. When it was my turn, I'd stand behind the square frame and say something like, "Last night my dad fell down on the sidewalk walking from the bus stop, and when he got home, his face was dripping with blood." Or, "Last night my parents were fighting, and the police came to my house." The look of shock on my classmates' faces was important to me. Would Mrs. Gill favor me for sharing this important news?

One day that summer when I was eight years old, I stepped off the bus after a long day at Camp Acquackanonk. It was confusing that our neighbor and close friend, Mrs. Conway, was there to greet me instead of my mom. She told me that Dad was in the hospital and that he was going away for a while. The word *hospital* was scary, but the fact that Dad was "going away for a while" was music to my ears. It turns out that he had gone to rehab at a local treatment facility. I had no idea what that meant, but it didn't matter. The only way that could have been better news was if Mrs. Conway had said, "Your father has disappeared, and he is never coming back."

We visited Dad one day for Family Day, and it didn't seem at all like a hospital. Instead of seeing him laid up in bed, we found him basking in the sun in a chaise lounge next to the pool. He seemed genuinely disappointed to see us, if not downright angry at the intrusion. I remember going into a room with folding chairs and listening to serious talking for what seemed like forever. Mom, my big brother, and I returned home and had a peaceful few weeks before Dad came home and all hell broke loose again.

Dad returned from rehab, and our family began attending Twelve Step meetings. Dad went to a recovery group for alcoholics, Mom went to a group for spouses and other adults affected by alcoholism of a loved one, my older brother went to a recovery group for teenage children of alcoholics, and I went to a group for children nine to twelve years old. The meetings were held at a local church, which was strange for a little Jewish girl like me who had never even stepped foot inside a synagogue, let alone a church. Some nights Dad went with us, other nights Mom went. (My younger brother was just a baby at this time, so one of them stayed home with him.) I can't remember all of us going as a family. We'd walk in together and then find our own group. Sometimes on the nights of "open" meetings (when nonmembers could attend), hundreds of people would gather, and the smoke in the air was so thick you could barely see across the room. There were always volunteers making coffee, and sometimes there was cake afterward, in honor of people celebrating anniversaries of their years of sobriety.

My first support group meeting for children of alcoholics was in Nutley, New Jersey, in a little playroom in the upstairs of the church. Several little kids were there, and a very nice, pretty lady with long blond hair and wearing a fringy scarf was our "sponsor." She helped run the meeting and keep an eye on us. The Preamble, the Twelve Steps, and the Twelve Traditions that set forth the "rules" of Twelve Step groups were laminated in plastic, and we shared the reading by passing the sheets around the table. We learned that these rules are read at the beginning of every meeting and that the Twelve Steps were our guide for living. The slogans "Easy Does It," "First Things First," "Live And Let Live," and "Think" were displayed in the middle of the table, with "Think" displayed upside down. We talked about our families, and for the first time in my life, I felt safe. There were other kids like me; there were other families like mine! Everything was going to be all right.

When I got home that night, I ran upstairs and banged on the door of the bathroom, where my mother was taking a bath. She begrudgingly said, "Come on in," as if she were already re-signed to the fact that she would be interrupted, and with that, I let myself in. At a mile a minute, I rambled on to Mom about the meeting and how much I loved it and how I couldn't wait to memorize the slogans and the Twelve Steps.

Even though we were supposedly a "family in recovery," life at home was still hell. Dad was a "dry drunk" for several years after he stopped drinking, behaving as if he were full of booze, though there were no drugs or alcohol in his system. For me, this was doubly frightening, because we could no longer blame drunkenness for his violent behavior. Mom reminded me constantly to be quiet around Dad—not to get him upset because it wouldn't be "good for his sobriety." I remember feeling resentful that the world still had to revolve around him; we used to tiptoe around him because he *was* drinking, and now we had to tiptoe around him so he *wouldn't start* drinking again.

Thankfully, I was already in "the program," where I learned early on about the "Three Cs." I didn't Cause my father's illness, I couldn't Control it, and I (or anybody else) could not Cure it because there is no cure with certainty that an addicted person will not relapse. A person in recovery, I learned, is like a person with diabetes. The disease is in their system, but they learn ways and develop skills to manage it and to avoid any triggers that would cause them to put the wrong thing into their body. I also learned how fragile a person is in early recovery and how difficult it is for them to stay sober. I now had a bunch of new friends who were going through this same thing at the same time, and we took care of one another. Forty years later, those friends are still dear to me, and to this day, *forty years later,* Dad has never had another drink. Over these decades, he has transformed into a wonderful and loving father, and he is finally a confidant to me. He has actually become an inspiration. But that is a story for later.

Back then, even though he was sober, I still often wished my father were dead. I had a recurring nightmare about Frankenstein coming to town that I wrote about as an essay in seventh grade. He was so big that when he walked down the street and put his left foot down, he'd squash a house on the left side of the street, and when he put his right foot down, he'd squash a house on the right side of the street. So Frankenstein squashed the houses as he walked down the street until he stopped at our neighbors' house, where I was hiding on their new porch that was just built in real life. The monster Frankenstein picked me up in his hand and looked at me. I was terrified, but he did not hurt me. He looked at me with his big, sad eyes and then put me down.

In an effort to respond to this obvious plea for help, my English teacher gave my essay to my home economics teacher, who also grew up with an alcoholic dad, and she pulled me into her classroom during study hall. Thinking she was doing me a big favor, this teacher said she understood what I was going through because she had gone through the same thing as a child. I didn't register these teachers' actions as concern or empathy. I felt betrayed and humiliated and marched out of the room and never spoke to them again about it. How the hell did they know about my problems at home? Did my English teacher call my mother out of concern about what I'd written? Did Mom explain that my father was a "dry drunk"? Did they plan an intervention?

### The Teenager Your Parents Warned You About

My eleven-year-old son is in the other room eating cereal and watching a movie on Netflix right now, and when I look at him and compare my life to his, it's hard to believe reality. At his young age, I had such adult concerns, and my childhood was long gone. He just ran outside to play baseball, and I draw comfort from the fact that he doesn't live in fear that one of his parents might come stumbling down the street drunk for all his friends to see. I also draw comfort from the fact that he hasn't come home drunk or high himself.

My diaries remind me that at age twelve, less than a year older than my son is now, I was drinking alcohol, smoking cigarettes, using other drugs, and worse. My parents didn't know where I was most of the time. Knowing all too well what trouble untended young people can get into, I fight the urge to hover and overprotect my son because he says he "likes the feeling of being trusted" when I leave him home alone to go around the corner for milk. I remind myself that my son is not me, that my family of the present is not my family of the past, that we have recovery tools and a better understanding of addiction than I had. Although I am far from perfect as a mother, these small signs of progress are reassuring.

Due to school district zone changes, I was sent to a new school to complete seventh and eighth grades. Most of the faces there were new to me, and for the first time in my life, I felt that other kids wanted to hang out with me. As a big group of us began to bond together, I worried constantly about fitting in, being left out of things, or being booted out of the group altogether. My mother wrote about this in her book *Adult Children of Alcoholics*:

> Feeling different is something you have had with you since childhood, and even if the circumstance does not warrant it, the feeling prevails....
>
> ... As a result, socializing, being part of any group, became increasingly difficult. You simply did not develop the social skills necessary to feel comfortable or a part of the group.[2]

Mom knew how I felt inside, but if she knew the danger I put myself in just to impress the other kids, she would have been devastated. She also would have been very scared to realize that, as with many children of alcoholics, the level of excitement and risk I needed in my life to not feel bored was dangerous.

On April 27, 1978, my diary entry reads, "I'm afraid that one day they'll just decide that they hate me and want to kick me out of our group. I'm scared shitless about that. Those people mean so much that if that happened I'd be just as well off dead."

It was late fall when we started meeting at a coffee shop next door to school called Fred's as early as 6:00 a.m. to drink coffee, eat chocolate donuts, and then go into the alleyway to smoke a few cigarettes and share a joint before school. The Polaroid photos of me and my other twelve-year-old friends are in an album on a shelf that I can see right now from where I'm sitting. I take a peek at them and find my memory of them is accurate. A wave of nausea comes over me as the idea of my kids doing what I did flashes across my mind.

On weekend nights, I'd ride my bike to meet up with my three closest female friends behind one of the liquor stores on Valley Road. We would wait for some lonely looking guy heading toward the back entrance of the store and sweet-talk him into buying us alcohol. We would give him enough money to buy us four pints of booze—Southern Comfort, blackberry brandy, Jack Daniel's, and Bacardi rum. Then we'd head back over to the school and hide in one of the outdoor stairwells. We'd open all four bottles and chug and pass, chug and pass, until they were all gone. I got drunk but never puked, didn't slur my words, and eventually, when we were done roaming around uptown, I'd ride a few miles home on my bicycle without crashing into anything. I'd walk in the door and have a perfectly lucid conversation with my parents if I had to, and then I'd go to bed and wake up without a hangover. For a little girl my age to be able to handle alcohol like that was not a good sign.

Lori's mom was easily manipulated and did whatever her daughter ordered her to do. She'd drop us off at the mall on the weekends for what we laughingly called our "shoplifting sprees." We would purchase a shopping bag for a quarter from the dispenser and steal clothing items that we could never afford until the bags were too full to close. Then Lori would call for a ride home. When I wore something stolen, Mom would ask, "Is that new?"

"No, it's Lori's," I would answer. She must've thought Lori loaned out a lot of clothes because this conversation happened so often that we'd both giggle (but for different reasons). One day we were in Stern's department store, and I had just placed a leather vest into my shopping bag when a woman from store security politely asked me and my friends to follow her to their back office. The police were there and took us to the station.

Julie's dad was the only one of our parents who answered the phone. When he got to the station, the police asked him to bring us all home. They gave us each a notice telling us when we had to appear before some board for juvenile delinquents and told us that we'd better show up with our parents or else we'd be in a world of trouble. Julie's dad barely said a word the whole way home. Why should he care? Julie was the youngest of eleven kids. His oldest two sons had been arrested a month ago for burning down a church, and another one had recently been shot. This was small potatoes compared to what his other kids were up to.

I got home that evening, and Mom was fast asleep on the pullout sofa downstairs. Crawling into bed next to her, I whispered, "Mom." She jumped up with that panicked look she always had in her eyes when she was startled awake. "What's wrong? What's wrong?" she asked. I started to cry and told her what had happened. She sobbed and sobbed, and I felt so sad for hurting her. We were both heartbroken.

Two weeks later, we went before the board, and they asked me questions and I answered them. I don't remember what was asked or how I responded; all I can tell you is that nothing came of it. Mom grounded me for two weeks and lifted the punishment the next day because I promised to turn over a new leaf. We never spoke of it again, and my father never knew a thing.

By the end of seventh grade, I'd taught myself how to drive Dad's brown Chevy Chevette. His spare keys sat on the shelf in the den perfectly aligned with his True cigarettes and his silver money clip. He left his car parked right near the bus stop that took him to work in Manhattan every day. While Dad was at work and Mom was wherever she was, I'd swipe the keys and take the car for a ride. I lurched around a lot at first, but eventually got the hang of it and became a pretty good driver. My friends were so pleased when I invited them to cut school and drive down to the Jersey Shore, only an hour and a half away. We'd have plenty of time to get there, fry in the sun for a few hours, and get back before Dad got off the bus and wondered where the car was.

It was an accomplishment not to get caught, as my father was meticulous about his belongings. Nevertheless, I prevailed until one day when Dad came barreling into the house demanding to know who had been in his car. I forgot to push the driver seat back after one of my friends exited the backseat of the two-door vehicle, something he would never forget to do.

Surely Mom had been instructed to deal with me, because he never said a word to me about it. When confronted, I vigorously denied that I had done anything to Dad's car. Then a few weeks later, my new boyfriend's mother saw me drive right past her on the main street through town. Talk about shocked looks! She called our house that night to tell on me, and Mom called her a liar and a whole lot of other things. Jimmy was forbidden to have anything to do with me. Unlike me, his parents kept him on an extremely tight leash, so that was pretty much the end of that relationship. A few weeks later, Jimmy dumped me for a new girl who had just moved into the school district. How could I blame him?

By the end of eighth grade, I was fourteen years old and

smoking a pack of Marlboro Lights a day, smoking pot almost daily, drinking on the weekends, and experimenting with whatever else came my way, such as hashish, opium, mescaline, LSD, and cocaine. My girlfriends and I would take the bus to Manhattan and go to Washington Square Park, drop a hit of acid, and spend the day people-watching in Greenwich Village.

In a parallel universe, I had aged out of the recovery group for preteens and moved into a group for teenagers, so I was now with the big kids who I had grown to look up to. I was shy and didn't say much. I wanted them so desperately to like me and was grateful that I had every right to be there and couldn't be rejected. It never occurred to me that others might care about me or even love me without me having to prove myself. They did and they still do. Despite my insecurities, I've discovered there is one thing for certain when it comes to recovery: There are no friends like those in "the rooms" (that is, in recovery meetings). You could usually call a total stranger from these meetings and ask for help, and they'd be there.

When I wasn't with my school friends, I was with my "program" friends at meetings. We'd all get to the meetings early and hang out outside the church, and afterward everyone would go to the diner. Or we'd go away for a weekend convention with hundreds of other kids in recovery from all over the country. Or I'd be at Tommy's house.

Tommy was my best friend in the program. He was drop-dead gorgeous, with long brown hair, dark brown eyes, a magnetic personality, and a contagious smile. The girls fell all over him, but I didn't have a crush on him in that way. He was a big brother to me. I confided in him, and he gave me advice. I would call him with a problem, and he would tell me to come right over, or vice versa. I'd hitchhike to his house (very dangerous!) and we would go up to his teeny-tiny room with tapestries on the walls and have deep conversations. There are things I told him in confidence that, to this day, no one else knows.

Tommy had three siblings and the coolest mom ever (his parents were divorced). Everyone in his family was in the program, and they were a hugely popular family. Their house was always full of people from "the rooms," and their house was just a special place to be. Over time, I also became close to Tommy's little sister, Danielle, and thought of her as the little sister I never had.

I was rarely ever home the summer of my fourteenth year. I was either biking all over town or taking the bus into Manhattan to party with my school friends or hitchhiking down to Tommy's house or going to Twelve Step meetings or conventions. I was a walking contradiction: drunk as a skunk and high as a kite half the time and in the recovery community the other half of the time. But as long as I was home by curfew, my parents were so preoccupied that they didn't ask any questions. Mom was at least concerned about me in her own way, but Dad didn't ask questions because he didn't seem to know I existed at all, which was fine with me at that time. He would've only gotten in the way of me doing what I wanted to do.

One night I was in the kitchen heating up pizza in the toaster oven when Mom walked in. She turned the fire on under the kettle and put a teabag inside a mug. We both stood there waiting in silence for the toaster oven to ding and the kettle to whistle. And then, catching me completely off guard, Mom said the words I'd waited all my life to hear: "How would you feel if I divorced your father?" I was so stunned it took me a few moments to speak. "Seriously?" I asked. "Seriously," she replied with conviction. Tears of relief began to stream down my face.

A few weeks later, my parents called my big brother and me down to the den that was the family room by day and Mom's

bedroom and office the rest of the time. Dad sat in his big recliner, Mom in the rocker, and my brother and me on the sofa.
Dad looked very upset, and his voice trembled when he said,
"Your mother and I are getting a divorce." And then silence.
And that was that—meeting adjourned. The emotions that ran
through me are hard to describe: relief that the nightmare was
over, grief that my family was forever broken, and shame because, except for Tommy, no one I knew had parents who were
divorced.

It seemed that, overnight, everything changed. To my surprise, I came home one day to find one of Mom's college stu-
dents there to "babysit" us for three weeks while she was away
teaching at Rutgers Summer School of Alcohol Studies. Did
she ever even tell me she was going somewhere? And Dad had
moved out. Did he even say good-bye?

Mom worked a lot and was at school a lot, both teaching
and working on her doctorate. Her private practice was getting
busier, and she began to go out of town on speaking engage-
ments. Now I went joyriding in *her* Chevy Nova while she was
sleeping until she caught me and hid the keys. I became known
for the after-school keg parties that I had while she was working and I was without supervision. I snuck out of the house
until all hours of the night and hung around with a bunch of
guys who were much older than me. They broke into houses to
steal jewelry, and one time when they were caught, I appeared
in court to testify for one of them to confirm his alibi. He told
the court that he could not have been at the scene of the crime
because he was with me. The judge looked at me and I nodded
in agreement.

I was even more of a mess by ninth grade; I was one person
with my group of friends at school and quite a different person
with my friends in the program, who were one by one getting

clean and sober and joining Twelve Step groups for people with addictions. Even Tommy had gone to rehab and was going to a recovery group for alcoholics. So instead of going to my regular meetings, I went to the open recovery meetings where my friends were. It was a crazy-making existence. I didn't believe that I was an alcoholic, but I wanted to be with my program friends. And when I went out to party with my friends from school, I had all of this recovery stuff running through my head. Once again, I felt like I didn't fit in anywhere.

The next couple of years went by quickly, and I was lucky to go to a high school where I made great friends who were "cool" and fun, but not self-destructive and looking for trouble. We did party a lot, but I rarely drank alcohol, sticking to "dry goods" such as marijuana, thinking that way I wouldn't become an alcoholic. My need for excitement and risk seemed to settle down a bit as I began to adjust to a happier life at home and more genuine friends. I never did get the attention I was looking for from my parents, so I abandoned that quest. Don't get me wrong—I took full advantage of the fact that my mother was out of town a lot and working a lot. But things were nice and quiet at home now, and Mom seemed happy for a change. I didn't want to see her hurt anymore.

When I turned sixteen and a half, I was eligible for a driver's permit, and Mom made sure I got one right away. Our neighbor was the driver's education teacher at school, and somehow through him I magically received my permit without ever having to take the test. He took me out for the required hours of driving with an instructor and told me to keep my mouth shut and not to tell anyone since he was doing my family a favor but breaking rules in the process. On my seventeenth birthday, I took the road test for my driver's license. It sure felt awkward to drive Mom to the test site in the car that I stole from her so many times, and I think it made her happy to watch me squirm! I passed the test, and as I drove out of the Department of Motor Vehicles' parking lot, Mom said, "Congratulations! This is your new car." I couldn't believe she'd done that. I thought she was nuts for giving me that car, and I remember thinking even then what a master enabler she was. But now that I am a mom myself and have walked in her shoes, I realize why she did it. If I was a legal driver, there was no reason to steal her car. If I had driving instruction, I'd be safe on the road. And if I felt like an adult because I had a car, hopefully I'd act like one, too.

It was the summer of my seventeenth year, and time for my favorite Twelve Step youth conference. I offered to drive anyone who needed a ride in my lime green Chevy Nova. Tommy's little sister, Danielle, was going to ride up with me in the afternoon because we wanted to get there early and everyone else was going too late for us. In the end, I ended up driving alone. Danielle decided to ride up later on with her brother and her boyfriend, Brian, who were caravanning with others who were headed to the retreat.

I got to the camp, checked in, and immediately regretted getting there so early. I didn't know a soul and was too shy to introduce myself around. I waited around for Tommy, Danielle, Brian, and the others to arrive. Eventually, I gave up waiting, went to my top bunk, and stared at the ceiling until I fell asleep.

Blood-curdling screams woke me in the middle of the night. I couldn't tell how many women were screaming and sobbing, nor could I distinguish their voices, and I lay wide awake in the dark, shaking, not knowing what was going on. Finally, I decided it was none of my business and convinced myself it was no big deal. Maybe they had seen a spider. Maybe there had been a breakup. Eventually, I fell back asleep.

In the morning, I learned that Tommy, Danielle, and Brian

were dead. Gone forever, just like that. My best friend, his sweet little sister, and her first love, gone. Three young, beautiful, happy, sober kids on their way to a recovery retreat. They were killed by a drunk driver who had fallen asleep behind the wheel. Others were also injured in the accident.

More than thirty years later, my heart pounds out of my chest and my eyes fill with tears when I recall that life-changing moment—the moment I knew my childhood was over.

--- TAKEAWAY ---

### Comfort Zone of Tension

Anyone who walks into a home where there is substance abuse walks into a place that is usually filled with tension. You don't have to hear a single word spoken. You know it, you sense it, you feel it. You have walked into a very angry, hostile place.[3] —Dr. Jan

Children who grew up in an environment that is fraught with tension and chaos are generally not easily stimulated. This was one of the root causes of my high-risk behavior. When you live in a home with addiction, you just kind of take everything in stride because you do what you have to do. It takes a lot to impress us ACoAs, and we don't find just any old thing exciting. I sought out things that were even scarier or more dramatic than what went on at home. When we children of alcoholics or addicts act out, we often do the most outlandish stuff because of our need for a high level of excitement and because we have to go to such extremes to get attention and/or approval from our preoccupied parents. It's also the reason why we as parents often take too long to act when our own kids get out of control.

When I was a very little girl, I was the perfect child, but that did not work so I escalated to very high-risk behavior. I tried to get attention from my parents by running away. They never noticed that I was gone. Then I tried shoplifting, but I hardly ever got caught. By the end of my "delinquency career," I was even stealing cars, and though I did get caught, my parents never followed through with any kind of punishment or discipline. Thank goodness I eventually got bored by this sort of challenge and went on to quieter things before I ended up in jail or dead.

In her work, my mother took note of the extremes in behavior among ACoAs. With us, it's usually all black and white and never gray. As children, ACoAs generally acted out or were very compliant. But the goal was always the same: to gain the approval or at the very least the attention of preoccupied parents. Too often, risk-taking children of alcoholics and addicts become impulsive, risk-taking adults. Here's how one person described this at that very first ACoA meeting Mom held at our house. Like me and so many other ACoAs, he ended up with his own addiction problems:

> Yeah. I'm a risk person. I have to take risks. That's the way my whole life is. When I got sober, I felt like I had to change everything within a fairly short time. One of the first things I did was to get separated. I also got a new job, and I got a roommate. I rushed to change everything because, for me, that's the way it works. I have to take risks. I don't know what safe is. I've known this about me for a long time—I have to have a certain tension level. I am never completely relaxed. I've always got to be out in front risking, doing something different, being scared, being anxious. It's like an addiction. I think it has a lot to do with my history and my own alcoholism. If there's a calm situation, I'll muddy the waters.

- Did you (or do you) have your own "comfort zone of tension"? Do you, like the person in the previous example, still find yourself creating chaos if things get too uneventful (which you might interpret as boring)?

- The next time you feel overwhelmed or think your children are out of control or going to the other extreme by trying to be too perfect, try this: Ask yourself if the tension and addictive behavior that runs through your family history is being repeated in your household. Dr. Jan would say that because you are aware of this, you have choices that you didn't have before.

- What is one small thing you can do to make your home a more relaxing place?

● ● ●

# CHAPTER 2

# Unwelcome Inheritance

Alcoholism is a disease. Being a child of an alcoholic is not a disease. It is a fact of your history, just like race or culture. It is part of what makes up who you are. There is no question that it influences you, but in and of itself it is not a disease.[1] —*Dr. Jan*

**W**e children of alcoholics are part of a story that began long before we were born. The story I am telling in this book is not unique to me or to my family; it is one shared by many who read these pages. It began somewhere in our respective family's history when the disease of addiction entered the body chemistry of our ancestors. It might be hard to believe that many of our personal struggles today can be linked to a disorder that affected the minds, bodies, and spirits of relatives who came before, but that is the story of alcoholism. That is the story of addiction. It is a true story with many chapters that evolve over time and across generations.

Might the fact that you have a difficult time teaching your children how to finish what they begin be related to the fact that your great-grandmother was an alcoholic a hundred years ago? Could be. The tangled web that is woven through the generations of families who have been scarred and changed forever by the unwelcome inheritance of addiction is strong and messy.

Although we cannot control its path, through education and our willingness to heal, we can minimize addiction's impact today and into the future.

To better understand the thread that runs through families where addiction to alcohol and other drugs has taken hold, we need to understand a bit about addiction itself. Whether we've been learning about this disease forever, or we're new to the recovery scene, it's always good to review the basics and learn about new discoveries. While my mother's work dealt with alcoholism and children of alcoholics, the acronym ACoA could just as well stand for "Adult Children of Addicts." My father's drug of choice was alcohol; your mother's or father's drug may have been cocaine or prescription drugs or heroin. Some people are addicted to more than one drug. Though the substance they abused may vary, the effects our parents' drug abuse had (and has) on us and our families make us members of the same club and beneficiaries of the same unwelcome inheritance. So when I talk about alcohol and alcoholism in this book, know that what I have to say pertains to other drugs as well.

## Alcoholism and Other Drug Addictions Affect the Whole Person

We can thank the founders of Alcoholics Anonymous (AA) for opening the door to our current understanding of how alcoholism and other drug addictions are diseases that affect all aspects of a person's life and being (body, mind, and spirit). Way back in the 1930s, they said that alcoholism wasn't about a lack of morality or willpower; it was an illness that could be treated in fellowship with other alcoholics and by following the Twelve Steps of AA—a blueprint for recovery that has been adopted and adapted by mutual help groups throughout the world whose members struggle with things from eating disorders to heroin addiction (and everything in between).

The National Institute on Drug Abuse (NIDA) defines addiction as "a chronic, relapsing brain disease that is characterized by compulsive drug seeking and use, despite harmful consequences."[2] If you identify with the list of characteristics of adult children of alcoholics (see the next section), chances are good that you have been on the receiving end of these "harmful consequences." As Dr. Jan said when she spoke to the First International Conference of ACoAs held in Toronto, Canada, in 1990, "It's no longer true that if your alcoholic gets well, then you get well, and if you get well, your kids will get well." In other words, we no longer have to wait for the alcoholic or addict in our lives to get help before we can help ourselves. And, because we now understand alcoholism as a disease as never before, it is easier to separate the person from the disease.

In the most recent edition of the American Psychiatric Association's *Diagnostic and Statistical Manual of Mental Disorders,* which mental health and addiction professionals use to diagnose various psychological conditions, alcohol and other drug problems are called "substance use disorders." This classification is broken down according to the specific drug or behavior, but each generally covers eleven criteria:

1. Taking the substance in larger amounts or for longer than you meant to

2. Wanting to cut down or stop using the substance but not managing to

3. Spending a lot of time getting, using, or recovering from use of the substance

4. Cravings and urges to use the substance

5. Not managing to do what you should at work, home, or school because of substance use

6. Continuing to use, even when it causes problems in relationships

7. Giving up important social, occupational, or recreational activities because of substance use

8. Using substances again and again, even when it puts you in danger

9. Continuing to use, even when you know you have a physical or psychological problem that could have been caused or made worse by the substance

10. Needing more of the substance to get the effect you want (tolerance)

11. Development of withdrawal symptoms, which can be relieved by taking more of the substance[3]

The greater the number of symptoms and behaviors checked on this list, the more severe the problem is thought to be, which helps clinicians determine if someone is a substance abuser or an addict.

As the following quote shows, my mother didn't differentiate between *abuse* and *addiction* if someone's alcohol use was significant enough to negatively impact a household.

Many people define the alcoholic as someone whose drinking or use of alcohol is causing a problem in any area of their life. Today we use the terms *alcohol abuse* and *alcoholism* rather interchangeably, although a person may abuse alcohol without being an alcoholic. Alcoholism is a disease that you may have inherited or you may develop—so it's not too relevant as to whether or not somebody is an alcoholic. It has to do with whether alcohol is getting in their way of being all they can be and whether their drinking is affecting the lives of others.[4] —*Dr. Jan*

Fairly recent studies in the field of addiction science about brain chemistry and addiction help us better understand the addictive behaviors listed earlier. In 2011, for example, the American Society of Addiction Medicine (ASAM)—an organization of more than three thousand addiction professionals—released a new definition of addiction, describing it as "a chronic brain disorder and not simply a behavioral problem." That definition resulted from an intensive, four-year process with more than eighty experts actively working on it, including top addiction authorities, addiction medicine clinicians, and leading neuroscience researchers from across the country. In an August 15, 2011, press release, ASAM quoted Dr. Michael Miller, its past president who oversaw the development of the new definition. He stated, "At its core, addiction isn't just a social problem or a moral problem or a criminal problem. It's a brain problem whose behaviors manifest in all these other areas."[5] And another of ASAM's experts, Dr. Raju Hajela, said, "The disease creates distortions in thinking, feelings and perceptions, which drive people to behave in ways that are not understandable to others around them."[6] Although people do not choose to have an addiction, just as they would not choose to have any other disease, such as diabetes or cancer, Dr. Hajela emphasized that choice plays a crucial role in getting help.

According to NIDA, addiction is considered a brain disease because drugs change the brain—in structure and in function. For most people, the initial decision to take drugs is voluntary, but over time drug abuse can cause changes to the brain that erode a person's self-control and ability to make sound decisions, all the while sending the powerful message "You want more. You need more." Our brains are made up of billions of brain cells that communicate by sending out and receiving natural chemicals that affect the way we think, feel, and behave. Alcohol and other drugs are also chemicals. They work in the brain by tapping in to its communication system and interfering with the way our cells normally send, receive, and process information. Most addictive drugs find their way to the brain's pleasure, or reward, center, where they flood it with more *dopamine*—a "feel-good" chemical found in the parts of the brain that control movement, emotions, thinking, motivation, and feelings of pleasure. It is a surge of dopamine that causes us to feel high. Some addictive drugs can release two to ten times the amount of dopamine we normally produce. When this happens over and over again, the brains of those who are addicted to alcohol and other drugs try to balance things by making less dopamine. Then they need more drugs to get their dopamine level back to normal—and even more than that to get high again. And without certain amounts of drugs in their systems, the discomfort of withdrawal tells them that they need more drugs just to feel normal.

Science has always been a painfully boring subject for me, but I found it impossible not to be fascinated by these new findings about our brains and addiction. The website for the National Institute on Alcohol Abuse and Alcoholism (NIAAA) has a treasure trove of articles on this subject that I couldn't put down, such as "Neuroimaging Identifies Brain Regions Possibly Involved in Alcohol Craving," "Teen Brain Activity May Signal Future Alcohol Problems," and "NIH Study Finds Chronic Alcohol Use Shifts Brain's Control of Behavior." Considering addiction in general and alcoholism in particular in this light gave me an aha moment of awareness: "My dad had a brain disease!" Merriam-Webster's online dictionary defines the brain as "the organ of the body in the head that controls functions, movements, sensations, and thoughts,"[7] and disease as "an illness that affects a person, animal, or plant: a condition that prevents the body or mind from working normally."[8]

Learning about brain chemistry and addiction made me further wonder: Can this knowledge help us understand why our parent(s) didn't stop drinking or using drugs even though they knew their actions hurt us? Quite possibly, yes!

In one of the very first group therapy sessions Dr. Jan held at her Institute for Counseling and Training, Mike, a member of the group, was beginning to see the connections between his behavior and his alcoholism. He said, "I've always got to be either out in front risking, doing something different, being scared, being anxious . . . It's like an addiction. I think it has a lot to do with my alcoholism." Consider if Mike were your father. How would his behavior affect your life?

The more I learned about addiction, the more I came to understand what the founders of AA meant when they described how alcoholism affects a person's whole being—body, mind, and spirit. Many recovering folks will attest to the fact that alcohol caused them medical problems, affected their mental health, and blocked their spiritual growth. In mutual help groups around the world, people share their stories about how alcoholism and other drug addictions have brought people to the brink of insanity or death and many of them to their graves.

Some people in early recovery might even blame God for their problems—their broken relationships, their lost jobs, their legal difficulties. On the flip side, those who have been in recovery for a time may share how much their physical and mental health have improved, and how their reliance on a "Power greater than themselves" is crucial to their recovery. They describe how, over time, their lives improved in many areas when all hope seemed to be lost. Their stories document how addiction not only affects the alcoholic or addict, but also those around them: family, friends, loved ones, and even total strangers.

I liken this to the drunk driver who killed my friends. I imagine him swerving all over the road, slipping in and out of consciousness. It was only a matter of time before he would hit another car and injure or kill someone. Perhaps there were other drivers who were lucky enough to escape the danger. They saw him coming and they had the presence of mind and the time to get out of the way. But Tommy, Danielle, and Brian just happened to be standing on the side of the highway because Tommy's car was overheating, and they could not escape. In my mind's eye, I see that my friends are terrified when they notice the drunk driver's car careening toward them. My other friends who were at the scene in a separate vehicle, including Tommy and Danielle's big brother, John, watched in horror from inside their car, and this traumatic experience is forever etched in their memories. Perhaps some of the other drivers on the road passed right by my friends' mangled and dismembered bodies strewn on the highway, and they didn't notice a thing. Still others may have seen this horrific accident in detail, and their lives were changed forever.

Imagine what could have happened if, instead of being arrested and brought to justice, that driver had continued on his way, oblivious to what he had caused behind him. Perhaps he would have hurt more people farther down the road, or he may have simply gone home and had dinner and fallen asleep in front of the television. Maybe he would have yelled at his wife and kids. Perhaps he didn't even consider the lives lost and suffered no guilt over the hurt caused—or he may never have a full life because he cannot forgive himself. It's possible that the victims or their families will forgive him and he will be able to move on. Maybe not. It never crossed my mind at that point in time and life to ask about what consequences that driver suffered, legal or otherwise. I heard through the grapevine that all he got was "a slap on the wrist." The truth is that no matter what happened or how that man was punished, nothing could erase the fact that my friends were gone—forever.

I imagine the paramedics coming upon the worst accident scene they had probably ever seen and how they had to function nonetheless. They had to assess the injuries of those who survived and prioritize what care needed to be given and to whom and in what order. Some people were treated at the scene, others went to the hospital, and three young people went to the morgue. I wonder if the rescuers' families asked them how their day was at work. Maybe they fell apart. Maybe they said they were "fine" because they didn't want to go through it again by talking about it.

Just think of all the people affected by the actions of a single drunk driver on that fateful day: the driver himself, his family, his friends, his employer; the friends who witnessed the carnage, and everyone important to them. The passersby on the road. Tommy, Danielle, and Brian, and their families, friends, and the communities they lived in. Their teachers, classmates, colleagues. The emergency responders. Think of all the innocent people who in some way felt the impact of that one person's actions. That is the power of the disease of alcoholism.

## Characteristics of Adult Children of Alcoholics

ACoAs know all too well that alcoholism is a family disease. That doesn't just mean that our parents' addiction influences the way we act or the way we teach our children. It has to do with our physiology and the way our bodies react, the way our minds react, and the way our spirits react to what we've experienced and what we've inherited. It has to do with how our body chemistry was passed down to us through generations and how we continue to pass that down to our children and grandchildren, and so on.

It is widely believed that alcoholism manifests itself in different ways. For example, it can affect the body's inability to metabolize sugar properly. My friend, the rabbi and author Dr. Abraham J. Twerski, shared observations he made about his addicted patients at a conference that we both spoke at in the mid-1990s. He believes that because of the way sugar is processed in the presence of alcoholism and the intergenerational nature of the disease, it is very common to have sugar addiction, obesity, diabetes, alcoholism, or another addiction in the same family. This means that if one of your parents has an addiction disorder, the risks for you having any number of addiction disorders are much greater. To make matters more confusing is the disturbing fact that if our grandparents are alcoholics, then, whether our parents were themselves alcoholics or not, we were raised by parents who were at the very least adult children of alcoholics with all the addictive behaviors that implies. So the effect that our addicted grandparents have on us can carry over into our adulthood as we live out the behavior that our parents modeled for us. Unless we interrupt the cycle, we inadvertently keep it going with our own children, and then we may often wonder why our households are so chaotic when we have tried so hard to be different than our parents. The tangled web of addiction is very difficult to tease apart and understand, but it can be done.

To do that, we have to understand how addiction also has to do with the *emotional* impact that alcoholism has had on our families and the hard truth that so many of us who were raised by parents with an addiction disorder had trouble sorting out—the difference between "child" and "adult." Here's an expanded version of a quote from Dr. Jan that appears in the introduction to this book; it helps explain what Mom observed in her own children and in other ACoAs who often seemed like children in adult bodies when they matured and seemed like little adults when they were kids.

> We refer to them as adult children because though they are chronologically adults, because of the environment they were brought up in, and the fact that they have really had to bring themselves up, in some areas of their lives their maturity level is more like that of a child than an adult. So there is an adult that became an adult too soon in some ways, and a child that didn't have the parenting that they may have needed in order to develop in other ways. Many if not most of the ACoAs that have come through our doors have come in with a presenting problem that on the surface may seem current, but indeed has its roots in the previous experience of living with alcoholism. They begin to gain an understanding of how their childhood experience has impacted them in their adult lives (and as parents). It is truly amazing to see the perseverance ACoAs have in terms of understanding themselves, regardless of and despite of the tremendous pain involved, especially for those who have become alcoholic themselves, and have to face that they have become addicted despite their promises to never become like their alcoholic parents.[9] —Dr. Jan

The first-ever ACoA group that Dr. Jan held in our living room put together the following list of characteristics to describe themselves. It is this list that spread like wildfire in the 1980s, bringing the book *Adult Children of Alcoholics* to the *New York Times* Best Sellers list for almost a full year. As the numbers of members of Twelve Step meetings for alcoholics mushroomed from hundreds to thousands to millions all over the world, their children began to realize that they, too, needed help in moving past the experience of growing up with an alcoholic parent. That early ACoA group agreed that adult children of alcoholics had the following characteristics in common. As Mom wrote in *Adult Children of Alcoholics,* "You may want to add to or modify my list. Perceptions may vary, but regardless of the differences, the connections become obvious."[10]

1. Adult children of alcoholics guess at what normal behavior is.

2. Adult children of alcoholics have difficulty following a project through from beginning to end.

3. Adult children of alcoholics lie when it would be just as easy to tell the truth.

4. Adult children of alcoholics judge themselves without mercy.

5. Adult children of alcoholics have difficulty having fun.

6. Adult children of alcoholics take themselves very seriously.

7. Adult children of alcoholics have difficulty with intimate relationships.

8. Adult children of alcoholics over-react to changes over which they have no control.

9. Adult children of alcoholics constantly seek approval and affirmation.

10. Adult children of alcoholics usually feel that they are different from other people.

11. Adult children of alcoholics are super responsible or super irresponsible.

12. Adult children of alcoholics are extremely loyal, even in the face of evidence that the loyalty is undeserved.

13. Adult children of alcoholics are impulsive. They tend to lock themselves into a course of action without giving serious consideration to alternative behaviors or possible consequences. This impulsivity leads to confusion, self-loathing and loss of control over their environment. In addition, they spend an excessive amount of energy cleaning up the mess."[11]

Mom always said, "Adult children as a group are more eager for help than any other group I've ever known." But as the recovery field began to expand beyond all expectations, and before she became ill in the early 1990s, she expressed some concerns. She felt that while ACoAs were initially excited and willing to learn about themselves, somewhere along the line their growth process began to stagnate. I shared her concern that some ACoAs seemed to be getting stuck in what looked to us like a comfortable place of blaming others for their lot in life. The more they identified with other families like theirs, their sense of isolation often diminished. They may have found a new social group, but their families of origin did not seem to be healing. This concerned us, especially as these folks began to have children of their own.

After the Adult Children of Alcoholics movement ignited, many support groups formed that modeled themselves on Twelve Step groups like AA. But they were not run by professionally trained therapists. In our opinion, this was a mistake. Unlike the Twelve Step recovery groups for alcoholics or drug addicts, where recovery is ongoing because of the ever-present risk of relapse, we felt strongly that ACoA groups should not continue on indefinitely. The philosophy of our clinic was that our support groups were a means toward an end. Our intended purpose was for ACoAs to understand our common experiences through sharing with others and learning from what others shared with us, so that we could begin our healing. In essence, our goals were threefold: personal recovery, breaking the cycle of addiction for the next generation, and—ideally—healing our families of origin.

While the ACoA support group may serve as a good substitute family for the purposes of this healing process, we never intended it to *replace* the family. (Extreme cases of abuse or trauma may be an exception, where support groups and other new relationships are often needed to replace a toxic family system.) Our goal was always to heal the family to whatever extent was healthy and possible. The way "recovery" was taught at Mom's Institute for Counseling and Training, ACoAs could salvage the possibility for happiness in our own lives and pave the way for our children to have healthier relationships than we did. As we practice this process of recovery, we create the possibility that when we have our own families, we will not repeat the past, but rather perpetuate this new legacy.

It has been such a gift to know that millions of people all over the world have benefited from my mother's work. But unfortunately, almost thirty years later, many ACoAs are still stuck in their "recovery" and may not even realize it. Recently, I went to a Twelve Step support group meeting for Adult Children of Alcoholics in my area. I was baffled by the discussion about "our disease" and how to prevent "relapse." Afterward, I introduced myself to the chairpersons, who were husband and wife. I thanked them for their service, and the wife smiled and told me that they have been running this group for seven years. Trying to conceal my surprise, I asked, "How long do people usually stay in the group?" She smiled again and said, "Oh, we'll be here forever. There's no such thing as graduation—this isn't going away." I'm not usually at a loss for words, but I was in this instance. If my mother were alive, she would've known what to say. She would've been brutally honest, and loving and funny and insightful, all at once—just as she was when she uttered the following words:

> Because you are an adult child of an alcoholic does not mean you are sick. Being an adult child of a dysfunctional family is a part of your history. It is not part of a diagnosis. Most of you want to change childhood patterns that are no longer useful to you. That's different. Children of alcoholics are set up for their struggles. You are not sick. You got set up. This was not your choice. Once you recognize that it happened to you, you now have a whole variety of choices about how to prevent it from happening to you again or to behave in different ways or to choose differently.[12] —Dr. Jan

### Codependency and Addictive Thinking

I don't remember hearing the word *codependency* back in the seventies, but the recovery group for children of alcoholics that I attended taught me what it was. For me, it meant that Mom needed a Twelve Step support group because she was so preoccupied with Dad's drinking that she didn't think about anything else. Or, as Melody Beattie explains it in her book *Codependent No More*, "A codependent person is one who has let another person's behavior affect him or her, and who is obsessed with controlling that person's behavior."[13]

One example of codependency that made a lot of sense to me was given to me during my substance abuse counselor training. The instructor first drew two circles next to one another on the blackboard to represent two people who were not dependent on one another. The second set of circles that he drew partially overlapped one another, representing two people who were interdependent, or dependent on one another in a mutual and healthy way. The third set of circles showed one inside the other, denoting how one person's life can be consumed by the other. This is the nature of codependency, where a person is so preoccupied with the other that they are distracted from their own life. As the joke in recovery circles explains it: You know you're codependent if, when you're dying, someone else's life flashes before your eyes!

In my friend Dr. Twerski's groundbreaking book *Addictive Thinking*,[14] he tells a story about a codependent husband who came to him for help. This man's wife was an alcoholic who had relapsed. Prior to this relapse, she had gone through detox at a hospital and attended several AA meetings when she was released. But then she quit going, saying those meetings were not for her. She told her husband she was different from the other people and believed she had nothing in common with them.

Dr. Twerski told the husband that his wife's resistance to AA was not unusual. After all, in AA, he said, she would learn that she could not drink again. Obviously, as her relapse showed, this was something that she did not want to hear.

Then Dr. Twerski asked the man how his Al-Anon program was going, and the man said, "I went to two meetings, but that program is not for me. I have nothing in common with the people there."

The good doctor pointed out to the man how he was parroting his wife's exact words, offering the same excuses for avoiding a recovery program that she had used.

As Dr. Twerski concluded, the anxiety about change can be so intense that people like those in this example contradict themselves without even realizing it.

This story points out how sometimes codependent people align themselves with their alcoholic in denying the need for help. But Dr. Twerski also tells this story because it is an example of something that alcoholics, ACoAs, and codependents have in common: the self-deception that is characteristic of addictive thinking. He says that in the same way that the alcoholic is obsessed with drinking and cannot resist the compulsion to do so, the codependent person is obsessed with how to control the alcoholic and cannot resist the compulsion to try everything possible to gain that control. He also says that the three most common elements in addictive thinking are denial, rationalization, and projection.

Notice how the husband in the previous story has a distorted sense of reality. He knows his wife is an alcoholic but rationalizes that Al-Anon cannot help *him*. He denies that he has something in common with the others in the group, which is obviously not true, but it is what he would like to believe. So he bends reality to meet his needs.

Bending reality is a skill many codependents have mastered. One of my relatives unknowingly married a man who was an alcoholic. They were both from a community where most of the marriages are arranged, and very little contact is allowed between the couple before the wedding. From their first day of married life, her husband sat on the kitchen floor and cried all day. She assumed it was because she was a terrible cook; it never occurred to her that his drinking might be the cause of his bizarre behavior. Rather than face the reality that her husband had a drinking problem, she just worked harder to become a better cook.

### Learning from Our Family History

When we ACoAs look at the tapestry that is our family history, we discover that there's so much more than meets the eye. While we cannot change that history, the good news is that we can obtain skills and learn new ways of behaving and thinking that can change things for the better when it comes to ourselves and our children and their children. And the tools we gain for healthy living can be used in many areas. Dr. Jan explained it this way:

> As a matter of fact, what we are learning is that many of the things that work for Adult Children are really a model for many other kinds of dysfunctional families: people who live with other compulsions, people who live with certain kinds of mental illness, chronic illness, army brats, kids who've been in foster care or adopted, many who live in profoundly religious families, and children of Holocaust survivors, who have very much the same profile as the adult children of alcoholics.[15] —Dr. Jan

Many of her clients also shared with her that their children tended toward hyperactivity, needed larger amounts of medication, had dramatic allergic reactions to foods and environmental triggers, and often were addicted to sugar. Understanding all the elements that are woven into the tapestry of my family helps when I fall back to wondering why I sometimes feel like such a basket case. I am the adult child of an alcoholic with my own addiction issues and life-threatening food allergies. My father's family perished in the Holocaust. (We don't know if alcoholism ran in his family or not.) My mother was co-dependent. On her side of the family, there are sugar and alcohol addictions and depression. Her father grew up in an orphanage, and several family members were Holocaust survivors. My first husband was from a profoundly religious family, and the impact of that on our children and me could be a whole other book. And, of course, there are all the issues surrounding my own parenting and the impact all of this has had on my children, plus the body chemistry they have inherited from both sides of their family. I hope that when you look at all that is woven into your own family history, you will gain new insight and hope for the future.

Mom talked about how ACoAs have no database for how to solve everyday problems or relate to others because of the way we grew up. It's not that our parents didn't love us, it's that they couldn't teach us what they didn't know. That's why it's so important to interrupt this cycle of codependency and addictive thinking and pass on the healthy things we've learned to our own children.

> When one parent in a family is an alcoholic and the other is codependent on that alcoholic, the primary focus is not where it should be—on the health and well-being of the children. Children should get to be children and adults should get to be adults. The job of the parents is to take care of the children so the children do not have to take care of the parents.[16] —Dr. Jan

---
**TAKEAWAY**

## Addiction Affects the Mind, Body, and Spirit

It used to be that we had the alcohol professionals and the mental health professionals. And the alcohol folks said, "Look, you have a disease of the body chemistry, and if you get off of the alcohol, the rest of it will take care of itself." And the mental health folks said, "Because you had a difficult childhood, you've developed mental health problems, and if we sort out your childhood, then the alcohol problem will take care of itself."

What we are finding with adult children of alcoholics is that both of these things are true. We can't work on psychological issues as long as somebody is abusing alcohol and other drugs. We find that working on adult children issues is usually more effective after about a year of sobriety. But the critical thing is to make certain that both things—chemical dependency and ACoA issues—are looked at.[17] —Dr. Jan

So often mental health issues and substance abuse problems occur together. Sometimes one causes the other; other times both problems exist regardless of the other. In either case, Mom thought the best way to get a proper psychiatric diagnosis was to abstain from substances for a length of time so that alcohol or drugs are not impacting mental health problems. Because both problems can be inherited, just like many other diseases or medical problems, it's important to know our family's medical, mental health, and addiction history.

It's also important to remember that while alcoholism is a disease, being the child of an alcoholic is *not*. Dr. Jan said that while some children of alcoholics may need therapy in order to work through serious childhood traumas, the children of alcoholics she saw were essentially healthy in body, mind, and spirit. She also stressed that resolving childhood issues is a normal part of most people's life experience, whether or not they are an adult child of an alcoholic or drug addict. Here's how she put it:

> The children of alcoholics I see are essentially healthy. I don't see them as any unhealthier than any other group of people. I think therapists like me have pinpointed them because we've learned so much about them and we've studied their behaviors in depth, and we care about them so much. I particularly care about children of alcoholics because I gave birth to a few of them, and I care about my kids being healthy and care about providing the best home I can in order for them to sustain health. I'm not saying they are unhealthy—but I am saying they have certain adjustments to make in their lives that relate to the environment in which they grew up. And further, what I am saying is that they exhibited certain behaviors as children that, in other contexts, we could have labeled unhealthy, but in an ACoA situation can be seen as adaptive coping behaviors

that serve a useful purpose. However, as adults those same coping behaviors are usually no longer useful and need to be changed.[18] —Dr. Jan

My sponsor says that the whole point of recovery is to become the person we were meant to be. I believe this is spirituality—becoming our true essence and living to our fullest potential. As a child of an alcoholic, my spirit was squashed, and as an addict, my spirit was blocked. Perhaps this is true for you, too. The unique nature of this disease is that it impacts mind, body, and spirit in this way.

- How has living with addiction affected your mind, body, and spirit? Are you the person you want to be?

- Do you believe that being a child of an alcoholic or drug addict is a sickness? Are you ready to let go of behaviors that are no longer useful?

- Consider what gets in the way of living to your potential. Think about what changes you need and want to make and who can help you.

● ● ●

CHAPTER 3

# A Look at Three Generations

It's always important to take a look at as much of the family as possible. In this way, we can get the best sense of what genetic or physical predispositions an individual may have, and we can look at what behavioral patterns have been passed along down the line.[1] —*Dr. Jan*

**W**e've seen in the previous chapter the importance of what Dr. Jan is saying in the foregoing quote—how understanding our family history can give us a better perspective on our own lives. Many of us accept intellectually that the way we grew up affects how we act and react as adults, but underneath it all we may continue to blame ourselves for what happened in our families. For our healing to occur at the next deeper level, we need to understand our lives in the context of a bigger picture that takes us outside of ourselves. How did our parents become the people they are? How does that knowledge help us decide what legacy we want to pass down to our own children?

It's not enough to grasp what we inherited from our parents; we need to look beyond them to their parents (our grandparents) and, if possible, to their parents' parents (our great-grandparents) to see what forces helped shape them as children, as adults, and as parents. Understanding their experiences and behaviors in this context can help us develop compassion for them, and—who knows?—we might even grow to admire them. Most important, with compassion comes the possibility of forgiveness and the ability to accept them for exactly who they are—the same way we want to be accepted. Even if you feel your relationship with your parents is good, there's always room to make it better. The bad feelings you may carry toward them can lessen, and the good feelings you have toward them can deepen.

> The alcohol education programs in our schools teach our kids what will happen if they drink irresponsibly, but they do not teach them about what happens to them if their parents drink irresponsibly. Just as we can find patterns of behavior in alcohol abusers, we also find patterns of behavior in those who are abused by the alcohol abuser. In my own classes, I have found that imparting this information is very helpful in reducing the burden of guilt on those children. If they see themselves in a way that doesn't threaten them (as part of a bigger picture), they can begin to look at their experience without blaming themselves for what they have been through.[2] —Dr. Jan

ACoAs who are parents are often "in between" generations, with their children on one end of the continuum and their parents on the other. As such, we are in a unique position to make positive and healthy changes in how we interact with our children, with ourselves, and with our parents. And in doing so, it is possible to bring our parents and children closer to us and to one another. How healing it can be to know that our own growth might be the catalyst of such a dramatic and positive change in our families.

### Mom and the Red Hat

As I've already mentioned, while my mother was not the adult child of an alcoholic, she did marry an alcoholic. She soon discovered that the dynamics of that relationship fit right into her previous life experience and the comfort zone of tension that she'd always known. She said she had always identified very strongly with ACoAs but could never figure out why. An experience she had as an adult with her mother helped her understand why she was so critical of herself. Mom was a perfectionist who felt she could never do anything right, despite her achievements and so much evidence to the contrary. The following story helped me understand more about ACoAs and how I am like her.

Mom was returning home from the most exciting day of her career—an appearance on *Oprah*! She arrived at LaGuardia Airport, where a few family members were there to meet her. Unfortunately, instead of the celebratory greeting she anticipated, she was met with the bad news that her mother was in the hospital in Queens, just a few miles away. She was instructed to go there immediately, and then bring her elderly father home with her so she could take care of him while her mother was in the hospital. It seemed like everyone was more nervous than Mom was, as they waited for her to react with shock, disappointment, high anxiety, and/or concern. But she only registered calm and competence. As she later explained, when you live with an addict, as she did during her twenty-year marriage, crisis becomes the norm—nothing much fazes you.

Grandmother was admitted to the ICU after ignoring a medical problem to the point of a crisis that required an ambulance ride to the hospital. I have no idea what the problem was, because no one told me, and I was afraid to ask. I just remember Mom muttering something like, "Sometimes we don't have to die in order to hit bottom."

I watched my mother collect her luggage at the airport baggage claim and then continue to the hospital to see her mother.

She got her visitor's badge, headed for the ICU, but stopped short at the doorway to Grandmother's room. She said it was surprising and a little frightening, actually, to see her mother in bed with all of the tubing and such, sleeping, looking so small and helpless in that silly gown. Usually, it was Grandmother who ran the show, but not today.

Mom stood in the doorway for a moment, taking in the scene and collecting herself before stepping inside. She knew that Grandmother would never want to be seen this way, hardly looking like herself. The world had never seen her a day in her life without her fancy wig on, but there she lay, with her own stringy, thin gray hair peeking out from under the hospital blanket. She had none of her usual makeup on, and she didn't wear one of the stylish suits she made herself because even Bloomingdale's didn't sell clothes that met her standards. Mom said it was strange to see this vain woman, who had paintings of herself on her living-room walls and airbrushed photographs of herself on her tables, now looking so vulnerable.

My mother recounted that Grandmother turned her head toward the doorway, with that sixth sense that we have when someone is staring at us from behind, and saw her daughter standing there waiting to enter. Without missing a beat, Grandmother weakly used her index finger to beckon her daughter to come close. My mother obeyed, nearing the bed, bending over to hear what profundity her mother had to say. And then, in a whisper that only they could hear, her mother said, "Janet, you really should be wearing a red hat with that coat."

My mother loved my grandmother to pieces despite her lack of tact, and so did I. There was something endearing and sometimes hilarious about the way she went through her life uncensored, even though she often said the most awful things! We could always count on Grandmother to tell it like it was (or how she imagined it to be), all the while looking fabulous. I was shocked when Mom told me that on her sixteenth birthday, my grandmother promised her that if she lost twenty pounds she'd get her a "nose job." Mom also told me that she spent her life trying to prove to her mother that she existed—that her brother was *not* an only child. As a youth, Mom excelled in school, was always in fashion, and played tennis like a pro—all in an effort to gain her mother's approval. But even as a grown woman with a doctorate and a successful career and an appearance on *Oprah,* Mom said she still didn't feel good enough.

As a member of the "third" generation, I unconsciously learned a lot from watching my mother twist herself inside out for her mother's approval. She continued that pattern in her marriage to my father, thinking that the drinking was her fault because she wasn't good enough. And I followed suit. If I weren't such a rotten kid, my dad wouldn't drink. If I were cuter and smarter, our family would be happy. I do not know the entire history of alcoholism on my mother's side, but I do remember that when my great-uncles were around, the booze came out, and behavior among the adults who were drinking got more boisterous and less inhibited. And, as noted before, I also know that sugar addiction and severe food and environmental allergies run through my mother's side—all maladies often connected with a history of alcohol and other drug addiction somewhere in a family.

Because my father's family perished in the Holocaust, it is impossible to say for sure what his lineage is, but chances are good that he was not the only one with a substance abuse problem. While I cannot trace for certain the roots of addiction among my ancestors, I do know that my father's alcoholism played a significant role in my life, and that, in turn, my own addictive behaviors affect how I parent. This is a reality I live with every day, but thanks to the insights I've gained from Mom and from my own recovery work, my children already know my story (and their father's story) and the impact addiction has had on their own generation and the two generations that came before them. I feel hopeful that this knowledge will help break our family's cycle of addictive behavior so my grandchildren will not have to endure a childhood like mine or like that of so many other ACoAs.

As my friend Jackie can attest, sifting through the sands of a family's history with addiction can expand the view we have of ourselves and give us a brand-new perspective on how we view the world beyond self.

### Jackie's Story

Even though she has been sober for four years, my friend Jackie calls herself "a garden variety alcoholic." If you knew her, she would tell you that she did not drink to numb her feelings or to avoid problems. She fell in love with alcohol during her years working as a bartender. She simply loved to drink and was not able to stop herself once she started. In fact, she acquired four DWIs after the age of thirty, and she is no longer allowed to drive. Following in his mother's footsteps, Jackie's son became addicted to heroin during high school and has been through treatment more than once.

Life became very difficult for Jackie. After a bitter divorce, she relapsed after two years of sobriety and was again arrested for driving while intoxicated. When court officials found out that her son had a drug problem, they made him leave her home. It was devastating for both Jackie and her son. Jackie judges herself harshly for being an alcoholic and especially for the relapse that made her situation so much worse. She says it put her in a position where her son was hurt, and that pains her deeply.

Jackie was raised in a loving and stable household where her parents never drank, and out of the four children in her family, she is the only one who developed a problem with alcohol. I asked her about her grandparents, and at first she said that they were totally normal; she thought she was just a freak of nature. But upon deeper reflection, Jackie began to remember incidents when one grandparent on each side of her family drank to the point of oblivion. She remembers how her grandfather on her father's side would often not wake up for holiday dinners because he had passed out drunk in his recliner. And she recalled how her grandmother on her mother's side became the life of the party after a few cocktails—which happened often.

Jackie asked her mother if her memory was correct, and her mother confirmed that it was. In fact, her mother told her that *both* of Jackie's grandparents on her mother's side were "big drinkers." Because her father's father simply fell asleep when he had too much to drink, no one thought that he had a problem. And because her mother's parents were so lively and fun, nobody considered them to be problem drinkers either. Jackie asked her mother how growing up with alcoholic parents had affected her. Her mother said that when she was growing up, her parents fought a lot and that she became afraid when they argued. She said that she felt embarrassed when they got drunk around other people and that she always watched what she said because she didn't want to anger either one of her parents.

Under this new lens, Jackie began to realize that three of her grandparents were probably alcoholics, which would make both her parents adult children of alcoholics, and that she and her son more than likely inherited the addictive body chemistry that runs in her family. Because her parents grew up in an environment where alcohol abuse was common, they made sure that their home was a peaceful and happy place. They avoided alcohol because the way their parents drank turned them off. So alcoholism seemed to skip her parents' generation, which is why Jackie did not realize that this disease ran in her family.

Having a wider view of herself as part of a family history has helped Jackie forgive herself for not being able to resist the compulsion to drink. She understands that it is part of her brain and body chemistry and not a lack of morality or character, which she says helps when she slips into blaming herself too harshly for her son's addiction. And she also understands why it has been so difficult for her to confront the fact that her son had a serious drug problem. She learned from her parents that "everything was fine" even when it wasn't, and she also learned to avoid confrontation, which is why Jackie did not acknowledge that her son was in trouble when he began using and abusing drugs.

### Breaking the Cycle: Johnny's Story

Johnny considers his life today to be a miracle. Both of his parents were what he calls "low-bottom" alcoholics and, as a result of that, he spent a lot of time with them in bars during his youth. Johnny had been a member of a Twelve Step recovery group for children of alcoholics for a number of years, but in some ways his troubles back then were just beginning. Both his mother and father lost their lives to the disease of alcoholism when he was a teenager. He was on his own from a very early age and, even with his history with recovery, like so many children of alcoholics, he still fell into alcohol and other drug abuse. Because he knew where to go for help and had a lot of sober friends, he got clean and sober with the help of Twelve Step recovery by the time he was seventeen.

As Johnny found out, history certainly does have a way of repeating itself when it comes to alcohol and other drugs. Like his parents, Johnny married young and had a tumultuous marriage that fell apart after the birth of his son. Because of the resentment that his ex-wife held against him, she moved far away with their child, and Johnny was not able to see his son for the first seven years of his life.

Johnny explains that during that time he did everything he could to show his son that he loved him and that he was there for him. He told me, "I had held on to the hopes of getting him back in my life someday and worked at being a responsible absentee parent. I paid child support, made phone calls, sent gifts and pictures, and always let him know that I loved him. I bettered myself to be better for him in this respect. When we finally did meet, it was very awkward, but I never changed what I had told him all along: that I was there for him and would always be. We had some very rough times over the next ten years, especially when he developed his own addiction to marijuana, alcohol, and other drugs, but I learned that consistency was key to not losing him."

Johnny was determined to break the cycle of addiction that ran through his family. His years in Twelve Step programs and his many years of sobriety taught him a lot about why his parents were the way they were and how their addiction trickled down to his generation. His self-image steadily improved over the years as he continued in his recovery, and his life improved. Sadly, his son's disease progressed over the years, during which time Johnny remarried and had two children. When his son called wanting to come stay with him, Johnny knew he could not enable him by taking him in, and he turned him away. He said that was the hardest thing he ever had to do as a father. He knew that to help his son hit his "bottom"—that transformational time when things have gotten so bad that an addict is ready to recover—his son had to feel the consequences of his own substance abuse. Johnny said he also feared putting his younger children and his new marriage at risk by moving his son in with them when he was actively using.

Johnny was, and continues to be, a consistent and loving force in his son's life, and four years ago this young man entered treatment and became clean and sober. Johnny has been in a loving and healthy marriage for more than twenty years. He, his wife, and *all* of his children enjoy a close relationship today. And Johnny's son married the love of his life just a few weeks ago. Something my mother wrote is relevant here.

> Inherent in this model of looking at the family is also a model for looking at children of alcoholics. Because for every generation that has passed along alcoholism, there must be children affected as well who live out those issues if not treated. And since so many of these children become alcoholic themselves (in part because of their physical vulnerabilities and the behavior they learn from their parents), we need to break this cycle.
>
> So it is not enough, for the long term, to treat the alcoholism itself. After a year or so of learning to live a sober life, for the long run it will be necessary to address the rest of the picture. Ask who else in your family has a problem with alcohol. The answer will probably be "no one," which means [you] need a week to think about it.[3] —*Dr. Jan*

Dr. Jan's insights seem especially on target for Johnny and all those like him who have lived her words—those who have worked so hard to break the intergenerational cycle of addiction and its devastating effects.

### Give Time Time

After my friends died in that terrible accident, the rebellious part of me also died. I just couldn't stop thinking about how they were sober and still got killed by a drunk driver on their way to a recovery retreat. This was beyond irony. It was a cruel trick that boggles my mind even today. It also scared me to death and made me realize how reckless I had been with my own life. I was plagued with survivor's guilt. If they were sober and still died, how was it even possible that I—who continued to get high when I wasn't with them—was still alive? The cemetery where Tommy and Danielle are buried next to one another was two blocks away from my house, and I went there often. I would sit next to the big stone and ask Tommy's advice about things. In my mind, he would answer me by reminding me that, "Feelings Aren't Facts, Li" or "Easy Does It, But Do It, Li." I still hear Tommy's voice to this day.

My life changed with my friends' deaths, and I decided to turn myself around. Switching into high gear, I doubled up my classes in school in an effort to graduate from high school early. Mom was totally supportive of the idea, although the principal was not. He said, "If we let you graduate early, everyone will want to do it," to which Mom replied, "So why not let them?" Gotta love someone who thinks and acts like that!

My efforts paid off, and halfway through my senior year, in January 1983, I received my diploma. Then I found a job in a restaurant, and I worked hard to put away money until I left for college. It felt good to use the spending money I had earned for my expenses during the year, knowing I was doing this on my own.

For the next ten years, I only saw my dad about twice a year—usually for Christmas and once during the summer. Even though he had been sober for over a decade at this point, I was still angry with him for the hurt he caused during his drinking and early recovery. In my mind back then, his transgressions were unforgivable, and the damage he did was permanent. Case closed. My heart must have felt different, though, because I never did shut that door completely. Here's how Mom would've explained it:

> Even though [ACoAs] may be angry with the alcoholic or the irritable non-alcoholic, they feel responsible. They hunger for the love of the rejecting parent and are bound emotionally. There is a feeling of guilt. The child feels that if he were a better person, his parent(s) would notice him. He also feels that there must be something he can do to get his parent(s)' attention and approval.[4] —Dr. Jan

When I was a senior in college, I wrote Dad a fourteen-page letter telling him all about what I went through as a child under his roof. It felt good to tell him what a horrible person he was and how he hadn't changed. I told him what a nightmare my childhood was and reminded him of some of the terrible things that he did when he was drunk. It was a mean letter, and it was meant to hurt him as much as possible. It felt good to get all of that anger down on paper, and I felt brave when I slid it through the mail slot at the post office. I was preoccupied as I waited for his response.

What I wanted was different than what I got. I wanted him to beg for my forgiveness. I wanted him to admit that he was a terrible person and had ruined our family. Then I would reject him the way he rejected me all of my life. Then I would decide about letting him back into my life. I'd show him! Three weeks went by without a response, and I told myself that we were severing ties. Then a postcard appeared in my mailbox at the college post office.

A postcard? A measly postcard? How could he possibly respond to a fourteen-page letter with a postcard? I turned it over and it read, "Dear Lisa, I'm sorry you feel that way. Dad." I was stunned. That's it? What was *that* supposed to mean? I don't know what I expected, but that wasn't it. Perhaps I expected a fourteen-page apology.

### Courage to Change

How much easier life would be if we could script it all ourselves, assigning the roles we would like others to play and having them recite the lines we give them. I expended tons of thought and energy on the letter I wrote to my dad, and I was crushed and angry when I didn't get the response I anticipated—the long letter of regret *I* would have crafted. A huge part of my own recovery has been letting go of such great expectations and considering that other person's point of view.

There is a reason why AA and other Twelve Step groups close their meetings with the Serenity Prayer and why you will see it in almost every room of my home—a reason this piece of wisdom is one of the first things members learn by heart. There is a certain peace in accepting the things *I* cannot change, and a lot of growth that comes from changing the things *I* can. I continuously ask my Higher Power for the wisdom to know the difference. Each time I do this I am convinced again that this prayer is the perfect rule for working through any difficulty in life.

One of the things we cannot change is the past, and when we let go of the hope that the past could be different, it's easier to make peace with it. We can't change what happened to us, but we can change our perception of past events and our reactions to them. Letting go of blame is the first important step toward forgiveness, but that is not where it ends. We can go further than that, opening our minds to the idea that the other person is also on a journey of growth, and opening our hearts to the possibility of reconciliation. Acceptance is more than a state of mind; it's an action verb, something we continually practice. I am the child of an alcoholic. I am in recovery for addiction, and I have many loved ones both in and out of recovery. Addiction is in our blood—our unwelcome inheritance. We cannot change the reality of what was, but we are changing what *is* and what can be. We acknowledge and mourn what has been lost, but we accept it and cheer what we've gained. Learning about addiction and my family's history with it has allowed me to move beyond blame and resentment to a place of understanding and support and—dare I say—happiness? This has freed us as a family to celebrate things such as my dad's recent fortieth anniversary of his sobriety. This is my hope for all who read this book. Life is short, and there is no time to waste!

Case in point is a regret that I am living with today. My mother's cousin Ellen passed away a few weeks ago. Ellen and Mom were the best of friends when they were growing up, and Ellen was my godmother. There were a few things that happened between Mom and Ellen that caused their relationship to change, so we didn't see much of her after that. Then Mom got sick and felt abandoned by her cousin and best friend. I felt protective of my mother, took on her hurt feelings toward Ellen, and "fired" her as my godmother. Many years went by, and after Mom passed away, there was really no communication with Ellen's part of the family. Many years of family life were lost. I invited Ellen to my second wedding, and she was nice enough to come, but I did not get time to speak with her. Our relationship remained severed. Then something unexpected happened about two months ago.

For no reason that I can fathom, I started thinking about Ellen and just couldn't get her off my mind. I had the strongest inclination to reach out to her—so strong that it overcame my resentment. I remembered her telephone number even though

I hadn't called it since childhood. I picked up the phone and dialed her number. I got her answering machine and left a message that she did not return.

A few weeks later, I felt another strong urge to reach out to her again. I found myself considering my part in the demise of our once-close relationship, something I had never done before. Until then, it was my opinion that she had done all of the hurting and I was entitled to the apology. After thinking this through for a while, I realized that there were indeed things for which I could accept responsibility. I wrote her a short note and apologized for letting so much time go by without being in touch with her. I told her that it was so thoughtful of her to go out of her way to come to my wedding and that it was wrong of me not to be in touch with her after that. I explained that shortly after my wedding, problems in my marriage steadily became worse and, in my depression and anxiety, I did not stay in touch with her the way I should have. I told her that if she ever was available to get together, I would meet her wherever was most convenient for her.

Another month went by and there was still no response. I concluded that she must be so angry or hurt that she still did not want to have contact with me. I had felt so justified in my anger, but guessed she must be even angrier. I thought about sending her another note. Perhaps I could tell her that if I owed her amends for something, I wished she would tell me so that I could make it right.

And then I got the news in an email that was forwarded to me from my brother that Ellen had passed away. It seems that right about the time I got the first prompting to call her, she had become gravely ill. By the time I sent her the written note, she required round-the-clock care and was no doubt incapable of responding. I had no idea that she was ill and that she was so near to death. The email said that her small funeral was to be in a few days and only a few "close friends and family" were invited. Unfortunately, that did not include me. So I've been praying that Serenity Prayer a lot these days, trying to accept what is too late to change, grateful that we both made our small but ineffective attempts to reach out to the other, but still sad that neither of us took the additional steps toward possible reconciliation.

I share this story as another example of how easy it is for ACoAs to slide into patterns of behavior that were set in motion decades ago—even after we've gained an understanding of the impact addiction has had on our families and even though we have recovery tools on hand. For crying out loud, my mother wrote the book that defined what being an ACoA is all about, and I still slipped into my ACoA/codependent behavior by taking on my mother's hurt and feelings as if they were my own. By the time I realized this, it was too late.

--------------------- TAKEAWAY ---------------------

### An Expanded View of Family

Thirty years ago, Dr. Jan wrote about the different models that can be developed to look at alcoholism within a family. For simplicity's sake, she used the most common example of a family that came through her office at that time as a starting point: husband, wife, and children.

> I am using this model to keep the ideas somewhat simple. As you will see, the dynamics operating within the alcoholic family system get very complicated very quickly. There are many models within this system that can be developed to look at alcoholism within a family. There is the situation where the wife is the alcoholic. Or the husband is the alcoholic. Or both

husband and wife are alcoholics. Maybe one or more of their parents are alcoholics. Or one or more of their siblings are alcoholics. There is the situation where one or more children are alcoholics. Maybe there is a lover or roommate or the roommate's lover. There is the situation where the child has left home physically but not emotionally. Since alcoholism tends to run in families, and since people often tend to marry people like those they have known, it is not unusual for the spouse of an alcoholic to also be the son or daughter of an alcoholic and for his or her siblings to be alcoholics. And since children of alcoholics are predisposed to addiction, they may choose something other than alcohol—drugs, food, gambling, religion, relationships—the combinations are infinite.[5] —Dr. Jan

It is important to recognize that since Dr. Jan's book *Adult Children of Alcoholics* was published in 1983, the concept of family has changed and expanded. There are more single-parent households than ever before. There are more parents in the workforce and more stepfamilies. There are households with two fathers or two mothers. So when we explore the influences in our lives, it's more relevant than ever to consider not only our genetic inheritances but also the impact of all of the people in our lives who may affect our environment and our emotions. Dr. Jan would stress that our own personal circumstances do not have to be identical to what is written in this book in order for the ideas within its pages to help you in your life.

Each situation is unique, and each person within it has their own special needs that cannot be minimized. Just shifting the glass does not mean that nothing else changes. However, many of the generalizations we discuss will work regardless of your particular situation. Because it is not outlined precisely as it affects you does not mean that the principles do not apply.[6] —Dr. Jan

- Think for a moment about your own family. Who is in it, and how are they related to you genetically or emotionally?

- How has alcoholism or other drug addiction affected each of the members in your family?

* * *

# CHAPTER 4

# Adult Children as Parents

Adult children of alcoholics are forced to guess at how "normal" families function, so they have a sense of self that can be so tentative. Making decisions and solving problems is usually very hard for them because there may not have been anyone around to teach them what they need to know about life, or about anything. So it is natural that parenting can be a struggle for ACoAs because we can't teach what we don't know. ACoAs may have the right answers but may not have the data to effect the kind of change they want. One of the critical parts in terms of developing and maintaining healthy relationships with our children is to know how to do it. Trust me, people would have healthy relationships if they knew how.[1] *—Dr. Jan*

**h**ave you ever taken a look at how your upbringing has impacted you, or how it is affecting your ability to take care of your own children? If not, perhaps it's time. If you have never addressed growing up with alcoholism, or have other addictions that you are not addressing, your ability to parent effectively is being compromised. Without the right kind of treatment and help, the ACoAs who struggle with their own addictions or have not made peace with the past cannot effectively manage things if their own children start abusing substances. If we are not operating on all cylinders, our kids are at risk. Just ask me. As the saying goes, "It takes one to know one!"

### History Doesn't Have to Repeat Itself

By the time I finished high school, I had tried almost every popular drug except for heroin. In college, some of my classmates got into shooting up, but sticking a needle in my arm was inconceivable to me, and to this day I don't know anyone who has ever tried it who hasn't gotten hooked. Throughout my four years of college, marijuana, cigarettes, and sugar were my daily drugs of choice. By that time, it was my opinion that alcohol was a waste of calories. I smoked about a pack of cigarettes per day and more when I was trying to lose weight because it helped to control my appetite. I told myself that as long as I didn't become an alcoholic, nothing else mattered, so I took great pains not to drink too much. During my last semester, I decided that after graduation I would give up smoking and drinking for good. From the moment I walked across that stage, I quit it all, cold turkey. That part of my life was over. Nowhere in my consciousness was the idea that I had an eating disorder, even though I constantly dieted and complained about being too fat. Just about all the young women I knew dieted, so it seemed normal.

For the next twenty years, beginning at age twenty-two, I was free of alcohol, drugs, and nicotine. When I felt like it, I went to AA meetings to be with my friends. Even though alcohol did not appeal to me, AA says, "The only requirement for membership is the desire to stop drinking," and that was enough for me. A lot happened during those twenty years, but I didn't drink or smoke anything. My mother was diagnosed with cancer, and I entered an abusive marriage, was blessed with two children, gained eighty pounds, moved three times, buried my mother (I was twenty-nine and she was fifty-five), got divorced, lost forty pounds, remarried into a second abusive marriage, moved, was blessed with another child, gained sixty pounds. When the marriage had deteriorated to the point where my husband and I couldn't be in the same room, there were nights when I found myself sneaking off to a bar around the corner to escape from my chaotic household and to have a couple of drinks—just to "take the edge off" so I could go home and face my life. It wasn't so much that I wanted alcohol, it was the only substance available to me. I quickly understood the allure of hiding out at the bar. Even though I didn't care for being at the bar, it was a place to be alone that was close to the house.

It didn't take a lot for me to realize that the potential alcoholic who lived inside of me was alive and well. About a month into this behavior, I became afraid and started going back to AA meetings. Even though I was only having a couple of drinks once or twice a week, the fact that I continued to do so *and* went to meetings was not a good sign. This is what I did in my younger days. History was repeating itself. My real wake-up call came just a few weeks later, when my son was invited to a birthday party that was at a bar/restaurant. All the kids were invited with their parents, and there was an open bar. I knew this ahead of time, and since the party was on a lake, I brought my Big Book along and planned to sit by the water and read it while my son enjoyed the party.

Like a true addict, I immediately forgot my resolve and my backup plan and found myself doing the exact opposite of what I had planned. I stayed at the party and sat at the bar with a margarita in one hand and my Big Book in my purse. This reminds me of one of the sayings I've always heard at meetings:

"While we're in here taking our medicine, our disease is out there doing push-ups!" Eventually, I did let go of the alcohol, and I recently committed to addressing my problem of compulsive overeating and the sugar addiction that began in my early childhood.

As time passes and I gain an even better perspective about the way I have lived my life, the ways in which I have passed down my unwelcome inheritance to my children become clearer to me. None of my children know me as a substance abuser, but they have all lived out the consequences of my addictive/impulsive ACoA behavior: the way I have denied problems until the point of crisis before addressing them, and the way I have numbed myself with food instead of expressing myself. I have done my very best to make "living amends" to them—trying to heal the past by doing better now and into the future. In the same way, I'm urging you to see those loved ones in your life who have hurt you in terms of their life stories. I'm working on forgiving and understanding myself in light of my own history and life story. As my mom would say, I "came by it honestly." She talked about how ACoAs have no frame of reference for certain things—and how to be a healthy parent is certainly one of those things. I love my kids and I know they love me, too. I've done my best with what I was given, and I'm sure you have as well.

Our loving maternal and paternal instincts have guided us part of the way. But when it comes to recognizing and acting on problems, we usually need help. Most ACoAs are crisis managers, not day-to-day managers. Some of us had other adults in our lives besides our own parents who had a positive impact on us, and we can draw on what we learned from them. But most of us have learned from our parents what *not* to do, which is useful, but that knowledge still doesn't teach us what *to* do.

## Adult Children Raising Children

Raising children is a challenge under the best of circumstances. Even parents who came from "normal" families are sometimes at a loss when certain situations arise. That's a typical response when we do something for the first time. The difference between those parents and those of us who are ACoAs is that we typically have no road map to follow. We do not want to replicate our family of origin, but our previous life experience growing up in an alcoholic household can leave us with a hole in our education when it comes to parenting. As Dr. Jan would say, we don't have a "database" to draw on. Coupled with that lack of information is the problem that many of us come from a place of insecurity and low self-esteem, and we don't have the problem-solving skills that are needed in daily life. As my mother pointed out early in her work, although we are chronologically adults, we ACoAs often feel like children in many areas of our lives. So in effect, we often feel like we are kids raising kids.

Many of us worry that our children will fall into alcoholism and other addictions, and we want to prevent that at all costs. We worry that our children may receive the unwelcome inheritance that runs in our families regardless of whether or not we have addiction problems ourselves. Following is a discussion of what to me seem like the most prominent problem areas that my ACoA peers have in common and have struggled with as parents. In the next chapter, ACoA friends whose children are actually in the throes of addiction share their experience and hope.

*Adult children who are now raising children want to have a happy and healthy family life, but they usually have no idea how to go about creating it.*

It's easy for ACoAs to see families that we think look happy and make assumptions about them: They probably don't have any problems, the parents are probably happily married, and their kids (who will no doubt become doctors and lawyers one day) are well-behaved. They are probably all close with one another and never argue. They can easily afford family vacations every year with their extended family—all of whom also get along wonderfully and have no problems. We might envy or even resent them, or we might want to be around them so we can figure out their secret to happiness and become "normal," too. While it's true that our ideal picture of these families isn't realistic, there is something we can learn about how we want to be as parents from other parents we admire. Dr. Jan had something to say about this:

> One thing that needs to be considered relates to the unhealthy family system. We know what we don't want, but it has been my experience that knowing what you don't want does not tell you what you do want. Saying, "That is not going to happen to me" does not tell you what it is that you *do* want to happen to you. To understand what an unhealthy family looks like does not tell you what a healthy family does look like. We need information! Chemical dependents and ACoAs need real information as to how to live their lives the way they do want, and this knowledge will help them break the cycle with their children. So the first layer we consider when we work with families is that they do not know another way. They do not have the information as to how to behave differently. They could behave differently if they had the right tools and information. How many ACoAs come from families where they sit down to discuss issues that affect the family? That is a foreign experience, as there is no sense of how to do it. Even before we get into the therapy issues, we have to have some idea of how to talk to one another, how to function as a unit. How do we do our part and let others do their part? This is one of the places to begin.[2] —Dr. Jan

Learning the nuts and bolts about how healthy families interact and how such a household might be run takes time and effort. The Twelve Step programs teach us to connect ourselves with people "who have what we want" and to learn from them. But Dr. Jan explains that we ACoAs often have a lack of a sense of ourselves—an identity crisis of sorts, which makes it difficult for us to have a clear vision of what we want. Once we have the information we need, we have choices as to how to use that information.

Perhaps standing up for your beliefs is a new idea for you because you have spent your life trying to do what you think would please others. How can we guide our kids if we're not in charge? How can we be in charge if we don't know what we think or feel? As we learn ways in which we can be stronger as individuals and parents, we need to practice putting that knowledge to work. It is an adjustment to go from one way of being to another—to go from a place of insecurity to a place of believing and acting on our convictions.

In Twelve Step recovery, we're often encouraged to "act as if," so one day I decided to act as if I were "normal." I drive frequently from upstate New York, where I live, to see my family in New Jersey. It takes roughly three-and-a-half hours. Before I became abstinent from compulsive overeating and sugar with the help of my sponsor, I frequently stopped at the rest areas along the New York State Thruway to get something to eat. On one particular evening, I made a pit stop and got in line at Starbucks. I was looking forward to a giant iced coffee and a humungous chocolate chip muffin. I knew it was a terrible choice, but it was a long drive, and I was tired. I figured the caffeine and sugar would give me an energy boost and keep me awake for the rest of the drive.

Standing in front of me in the line was a woman who I thought looked "perfect." She was a little shorter than me (I'm 5 feet 3 inches), and she had a petite little body. She didn't have a hair out of place, and her pants and blouse were creased in all the right places. I wondered what this person was going to order, and I thought it would be interesting to do what she did just to see what a "normal" person would order at Starbucks.

To my disappointment she ordered a small cup of tea and a little package of three tiny shortbread cookies. That was *not* what I had in mind! But I went ahead with my experiment, ordered the same thing as she did, and headed back to my car. Surely it took that perfect woman half an hour to eat those little cookies, but not me. I didn't even remember eating them and then asked myself, "Where did they go?" And the tea was sufficient, but a far cry from the mammoth-size iced coffee fix I had so looked forward to.

I remember thinking how far apart that woman and I were in terms of what it took to satisfy that desire that we both had while in that line. I assumed that what she ordered was "normal," and I knew that my craving was out of bounds. Could I ever be like her? What would it take?

While that story might not seem to have anything to do with healthy families and parenting, I assure you that it does. For me, it was a lesson about how a healthy person behaves, and it gave me an idea of how far off the mark I was. It gave me a chance to compare my behavior to that of another person who "had what I wanted." If my children learn from my actions, what does it say to them when I order far more than I need and try to give them the impression that my behavior is normal? Not to mention the fact that I was chasing a caffeine and sugar high. This is one of the subtle ways that we may pass down our unwanted inheritance without even being aware of it. Copying that woman's behavior was a great lesson for me that I think of often. Look around you for examples of what you want to bring into your life. Talk to people who have what you want and ask them how they got it.

*Adult children of alcoholics who are now raising children often have difficulty with long-term and short-term planning and organization.*

My mother often talked about ACoAs' inability to plan and complete a task:

> Adult children of alcoholics often have difficulty completing projects and following routines. They can get very enthusiastic about something, begin the project, and somewhere down the line it gets lost. What experience do they have with things being followed through—where something was started and finished? More likely in the alcoholic homes they grew up in, a thing was not started at all or it was just forgotten.
>
> One of the things that was terribly important to us in the camp we ran last summer for children of alcoholic parents was the notion that whatever we started we would finish. The children were a little thrown off by this because most of them had no expectation that they could finish what they started. This also has a lot of implications for schools. Kids start a project but don't finish. What have they seen, what frame of reference in terms of completing something that one starts? And this is carried into adulthood and they don't understand, "Why is it that I can't follow through with something?" You can't follow through because you haven't had the model.[3] —*Dr. Jan*

Not being able to start or finish a project impacts school and day-to-day living. What sort of routine were you taught in your family of origin? Did you have meals at certain times, or did you grab whatever was available when you realized you were hungry? Did you have a consistent bedtime routine? Did your parents remind you to take your vitamins every day and brush your teeth before you went to bed? When you had a big project due for school in two weeks, who helped you complete it one step at a time? How did you stay organized for school? Did your belongings have a place, or did it all go in a pile on the floor? Did you have any idea what was going to be happening on a regular basis, or was everything a last-minute surprise? As Mom explained, a lack of routine and follow-through are common traits among ACoAs, so she urged them to be gentle with themselves as they gain and practice the skills they need to change these behaviors.

> Nobody was there to teach you how to do things systematically, so you learned to do things from crisis to crisis. So always be aware of that when you decide that you're crazy (which is probably on the average of once a day!). It may be because nobody gave you the information you needed in order to accomplish what you wanted to do. I can't emphasize that enough. Have I emphasized that enough? Okay.[4] —Dr. Jan

Because we were raised with this lack of consistency, we ACoAs tend to have poor self-discipline and difficulty developing and following a routine for any length of time. If you grew up in chaos like I did, perhaps you, too, are most productive under pressure. If I have six months to do something, I still don't get it done until the last minute. I have had to work hard at learning to plan and organize, and I did not do a good job at teaching this to my children. I am a gifted crisis manager, but on a day-to-day basis, it's quite hit and miss. In other words, life skills are different than survival skills. If you grew up with alcoholism as a "member" of your household, you may need to practice consistency and routine in order to restore order and eliminate chaos in your life so you can teach the importance of organization and consistency to your kids.

*Adult children of alcoholics can be expert liars and often inadvertently teach their kids the same thing.*

Dr. Jan explains how lying is a common behavior in an alcoholic home that can be passed down to children:

> The difficulties in building a healthy self-concept are obvious. The differences that I found in my research with children from alcoholic homes and a control group had to do with a distorted reality perception. Confusion as to who one is is part of the developmental process, but these youngsters [from alcoholic homes] lose a sense of truth. Lying is a way of life and, not unlike their parents, they often are not aware that they are lying. My concern is less with the lying itself but more for the lack of awareness. Choice does not exist unless there is awareness. Intelligent choices require education.[5] —Dr. Jan

We may have lied with the best of intentions, but, as my mother pointed out, there can be repercussions that are *not* intended when lying becomes the norm.

> Those who live with alcoholism have very little sense of what the truth is. They hear the nonalcoholic parent lying to cover up for the alcoholic—"John can't come to the office today; he has the flu." They witness repeated broken promises from the alcoholic—"I'll be home at six for dinner." Children learn to cover up because they don't know what will happen if they tell the truth.
>
> Trust means honesty, and honesty means that the other parent will say what he means and mean what he says and that you will say what you mean and mean what you say. It means that you can trust that the other person will not deliberately lie to you and that you will not deliberately lie to that other person. This helps to give substance to the relationship. This helps you know that when you put your hand on that shoulder, your hand will touch a solid arm. It means that it won't be "fly by night," and you won't have to be confused. It means stability. It

means that tomorrow's behavior will be similar to yesterday's. It means that you can count on things. It means that you can plan. It means that there is certainty about the other person and about the relationship. It means you can know that if you had plans to go somewhere on Saturday, that when Saturday comes, you will be able to go there. This is probably very inconsistent with your childhood experiences.[6] —Dr. Jan

Lying may have even helped us survive.

If you lied as a child, you are not a pathological liar if you are still lying as an adult. It's a habit that was useful to you as a child. It's not what made you crazy—it's probably what made you sane.[7] —Dr. Jan

But in adulthood these automatic lies can snowball, causing more problems than the original problem.

Adult children of alcoholics lie when it would be just as easy to tell the truth. [It] seems to be an automatic response. What's in it to tell the truth? The reality perceptions get distorted, so we find this a lot. So they have to cover up for the lie, and then what if they forget the lie in the first place? I think that's the biggest difficulty with lying—you have to remember what you said. But this is one of the things we see happening. And the lying has very little feeling involved, so you can't really tell if this person is lying. They can say something to you directly and you know it's not the truth, but since there's so little affect, since they're so conditioned to do it, you start to doubt your own senses.[8] —Dr. Jan

Because it can become an "automatic response," lying is a behavior that we might model for our children without even being aware that we are doing it. Take note of how often you tell a "little white lie" with the best of intensions. Consider whether it was necessary or not, and whether you did it out of habit.

Then consider whether it is something that you think is healthy for your children.

I became aware that sometimes I lied in an attempt to prevent another person from getting angry with me. For example, I may have told my husband that I went to the grocery store when I really had coffee with a friend, worried that he might get angry that I was socializing. Or maybe I gave my boss a dramatized reason for needing a day off when I could have just said, "I need today off." Sometimes I would lie thinking it would spare another person from hurt feelings. This is a habit I developed in childhood in an effort to appease my father so he would not get angry. It's a sign of our recovery as a family that Dad gave me this great piece of advice several years back, which I hope you can use, too. He said that if I say what I need to say in a caring and respectful way, then I am not responsible for the other person's reaction. They can jump up and down, stand on their head, or scream and yell until the cows come home. That's their stuff, not mine. It feels much better to be honest even in the little things, because the size of the lie doesn't make it less of a lie. It feels much better to me that my children see their mother as an honest person rather than the accomplished liar I know all too well how to be. It means that I am raising them to be trustworthy, too.

*Adult children raising children often blame themselves for their kids' behavior instead of holding their children accountable for their own behavior.*

Taking the blame for our children's mistakes is another carryover from our childhood in an alcoholic home. Many of us blamed ourselves for our parents' drinking and felt that if we were better kids, our mother or father wouldn't drink. Now we think that if we were better parents, our children wouldn't get into trouble. We think that everything they do, good and bad, reflects upon us. It can be difficult to sort out where we missed the mark as parents and when to hold our kids accountable. It is usually easier for us to blame ourselves than to acknowledge that our children are in trouble, especially if that trouble has to do with substance abuse. It is also sometimes more comfortable for us to beat ourselves up than to confront our kids.

My older children were two and three years old when Mom passed away. It was the biggest thrill of her life to be with them. She was in the delivery room when my daughter Rebecca was born, and she was the first person to ever lay eyes on her. I can still hear the joy in her voice as she cried, "It's a girl!" And the last time I ever saw Mom smile or heard her laugh, she was looking at my son Michael, who was smiling right back at her. These memories mean the world to me. Over the years, I've wished so many times that we could go visit their grandma or that I could call her for advice. Many times, though, I know what Mom would say—because she said it to me. And other times, I stumble upon advice written in her own words.

> Children need to take responsibility for their own behavior. If your child breaks a window, it is his responsibility to figure out a way to replace it. His failures are his, and his successes are his. Learning to manage difficulties is part of building self-esteem. Think about the things that help make you feel more worthy. Offer these things to your children. Self-esteem does not change as one grows older without hard work. Work at it as a family. You suffered as a family divided by alcoholism. Now recover as a family—united because of alcoholism.[9] —Dr. Jan

When I told my friend Leslie what a horrible mother I have been, she said, "You never woke up a day in your life and wondered how you could hurt your kids that day. Maybe you weren't a perfect mother, but you are a *good enough* mother." I haven't been the best disciplinarian in the world, but my kids know right from wrong. Whether it's a broken window or trouble related to substance abuse, if I stand in the way of them facing the consequences, it is the same thing as enabling them to continue on that path. It sounds cliché to say, "It's for their own good," but think of it this way—when we take on responsibility for our children's actions instead of letting them be accountable, it will take them longer to change their behavior. Why lower their bottom when we can raise it?

*Adult children raising children frequently look to others, including their kids, to tell them whether they are doing a good job.*
As ACoAs, our lack of confidence in our parenting abilities often prevents us from being in charge of our kids. When we measure our success as parents by our children's opinion of us, it is they who are running the show.

ACoAs often worry a lot about whether others like us, including our children and their peers. To this end, we put far too much effort into keeping our children entertained and happy at all times, even when experiencing a hardship or discomfort may be in their best interest. We too often mistakenly equate happy children with healthy parenting and "fun" for "happiness."

Bill G., a member of Dr. Jan's first Adult Children of Alcoholics group in 1981, in expressing his frustration with this part of himself, said:

> I would like not to have that need. I would like to wean myself off of that need to constantly seek approval for everything I do. It's a pain in the ass and it occupies a lot of my time. I'm constantly playing

for the audience, even my kids, and I have to wonder about that in myself, too. I wonder about struggling in front of audiences that approve of people who are trying to come together to work on themselves, because I'm sure I know that generates approval, and the thought has occurred to me that maybe sometimes what I'm doing is a sophisticated mechanism for soaking in approval.

Because so many of us ACoAs have a lack of conviction and confidence in our parenting abilities, we usually do not set clear boundaries, limits, or consequences, which translates into permissiveness. When we fail to set boundaries, our kids can interpret our wishy-washiness as permission to do whatever they want. For example, if you don't tell your daughter you expect her to be home by 11:00 p.m., she may decide she can stay out until 2:00 a.m. If you have a rule that "alcohol and other drugs are not allowed" but don't express it clearly, your kids may interpret your lack of clarity about this as you being okay with them using—especially if you don't deliver consequences. This insecure parenting style can send an unintended message to our children that there are no boundaries, and when they push the limits even further, we become even more uncomfortable.

*Adult children raising children tend to tolerate abuse or unacceptable behavior from their children rather than putting a stop to it because ACoAs usually fear confrontation and they question their own perceptions.*

We ACoAs often have to be hit over the head before we know for sure that the way we see something is actually the way it is. ACoA parents are often afraid of having their kids angry with them, so we twist ourselves inside out in order to please everybody in order to avoid negative feelings toward us. As Mom has noted, we usually have a fear of confrontation so we attempt to avoid raised voices, anger, and violence at all costs.

> Many children of alcoholics will go to great length in order to be people pleasers, a trait that comes from a variety of places. They want to be liked and assume that if they do not please the other person, they will not be liked. A second place that it comes from is fear of conflict. They think, "I will please you because I do not want to enter into any conflict with you. I don't want to do anything that will make you angry, because then I have to deal with that, and I would rather not deal with that." And thirdly, with many children of alcoholics it comes from a difficulty with making decisions. If asked, "Where do you want to go for dinner?" a child of an alcoholic might respond, "Well, I don't know. I'll go wherever you want." Back and forth and back and forth the conversation goes, and quite often it comes from a lack of making decisions. In parenting especially, this is a slippery slope.[10] —*Dr. Jan*

*Adult children of alcoholics usually have a high tolerance for physical and emotional pain and can inadvertently diminish their children's pain as a result.*

At the age of twenty-six, Gabriella married a man who was very assertive about wanting to marry her. Many years later, she was able to see that she got married despite her family's concerns about his need to be in control because of her low self-esteem and the underlying feeling that no one else would want to marry her. Although the abuse began almost immediately after the wedding, she was not fazed by it because it did not hold a candle to what she experienced as a child. She and her husband had three children, and the abuse escalated for the next several years until she finally left the marriage. The psychiatrist who evaluated the family for court said of Gabriella, "It took her far too long to marshal her forces once she knew the situation was hopeless." This is quite typical of ACoAs—rather than remove themselves from situations that are toxic, they learn to tolerate them. This is what we learned growing up in a household where we were powerless over our environment and had no choice but to endure it.

While this may be a survival skill in an ACoA's youth, it can backfire when we become parents. We might tolerate behavior in our children that might very well be unacceptable, or perhaps we allow it to continue past the point where we can intervene effectively.

*Adult children of alcoholics can become so accustomed to crisis that we run the risk of teaching our children to just "live with it" rather than change it.*

Many ACoAs tend to unconsciously re-create the uncomfortable, anxiety-ridden place that we are used to because it is familiar. Many times we do not recognize a crisis until it is at a critical point because that's what it takes to grab our attention. As Mom noted, this behavior is like an addiction unto itself.

> One of the first talks I did was at an addictions conference in Montreal on Families and Children of Alcoholics. I think we were in a Holiday Inn. It was a building that had twenty-six stories, and I remember very vividly that during this conference there was a fire in the building. Nobody moved. It was fascinating. Here it was during the break, the fire alarm went off, and everybody just drank their coffee. Finally, somebody came up and said, "You have to evacuate the building." So we very compliantly did what we were told to do and took our coffee and left the building.
>
> When the all clear sounded and we came back in and went back upstairs, I said, "You gave yourselves away. Because folks who did not come from an alcoholic or dysfunctional system like this would consider a hotel fire a crisis." But if you grew up

like this, you may not notice the fire unless the flame is licking at your feet.[11] —Dr. Jan

*Adult children of alcoholics and their children are susceptible to addiction, dramatic food allergies, and environmental allergies, and many are hyperactive and/or impulsive and diagnosed as having ADHD or as having PTSD.*

As has already been emphasized in previous pages, our unwanted inheritance is passed down to us in two ways: through body chemistry and through our home environment. When these two elements are combined, the results can be chaos. My mother recognized this early on:

> It's always important to take a look at as much of the family as possible. In this way, we can get the best sense of what genetic or physical predispositions an individual may have, as well as what behavioral patterns have been passed along down the line. If alcoholism, diabetes, hypoglycemia, or other sugar-related disorders appear elsewhere in the family, it may be a clue to understanding the cause underlying a particular client's addiction to alcohol as well as the child of an alcoholic's potential for becoming alcoholic themselves. We see so many children of alcoholics who are allergic, have PMS, are addicted to sugar—much greater than the norm. This supports the notion that the impact of parental alcoholism begins in the womb and that children of alcoholics inherit the body chemistry of their alcoholic parents.[12] —Dr. Jan

When we add our body and brain chemistry to our problems at home, our everyday life is bound to be affected.

> It is hard for the child of an alcoholic to develop a good attention span or to concentrate on schoolwork when he is concerned about what is going on at home or if he's been kept up most of the night by an alcoholic parent. The model child more often

than not will develop physical symptoms and will fall apart at a later stage. The child working below potential can be taught ways to compensate healthfully. The child can be taught to deal with stress. The child can be taught ways to increase his concentration, once absolved of his guilt for the family atmosphere. Tutoring, a healthy role model, and an understanding of the alcoholic family system can provide enormous support for these children.[13] —*Dr. Jan*

As Dr. Jan explained, taking care of our bodies and getting the support that we need is a good starting place for recovery.

A place to begin is to make sure that a child of an alcoholic is eating properly. Let's get off that sugar. Let's eliminate the mood swings. Let's use supplements, especially B complex, to manage stress. Let's learn how to get in touch with feelings when they are at the first stage of discomfort so you cannot do anything to compound these issues. Get involved in an exercise program. Not in an addictive way but in a way that is useful to you. Exercise is a terrific way to release rage. As one adult child told me, "Every hour in the gym allows me to let go of an hour of the rage I've held on to all of my life." All of these adjuncts to the therapeutic process are absolutely essential in helping someone live a healthy life. For an alcoholic who wants to get sober, or for a child of an alcoholic who is aware of the chemistry they have inherited and all that implies, good nutrition, exercise, and other self-care is the basis of addressing and working with the challenges of our own basic constitution.[14] —*Dr. Jan*

——————— TAKEAWAY ———————

## Remember to Focus on the Positive

Adult children of alcoholics usually judge themselves very harshly. If anything is wrong, they often feel wholly and completely responsible. When this happens, there is no way they can possibly meet the standards of perfection that they have internalized, and they keep falling short of the mark they have set for themselves. This can go on and on, and it doesn't serve a healthy purpose.[15] —*Dr. Jan*

It's so important for us ACoAs to focus on what we do right and to treat ourselves with care and respect. My childhood has taught me that I can get through anything. My ability to remain cool, calm, and collected in an emergency has served me well in my career—and in my role as a parent. I hope I have modeled a strong work ethic for my kids and have shown them how to be caring and patient and loving and loyal and honest and trustworthy. I love them for exactly who they are. Dr. Jan saw that ACoAs have so many unique and special qualities—she just wished we would give ourselves more credit.

Although their issues are very serious, there are many things that ACoAs can accomplish that many others cannot. So often we don't give them enough credit—either as children or as adults. It is my experience that ACoAs are extremely intelligent, loyal, and trustworthy. They can accomplish a whole lot, and they offer a whole lot. They will frequently accomplish a task that everybody else thought was impossible. Society benefits greatly from ACoAs because they can contribute so much. But too often they just don't feel good about what they've accomplished, so we need to recognize this. We need to stress that the idea is not just to get through something; the idea is to acknowledge, "This is who we are. We may be different, and there may be some aspects of ourselves that we choose to change or hang on to if they are useful to us." The idea is for them to become comfortable with who they are.[16] —*Dr. Jan*

We ACoAs deserve more than to just get through life. We need to practice being more positive.

- Do you know people who constantly put themselves down? How do you feel when you listen to them doing that? (It makes me feel terrible! I often tell them something like, "Stop talking about my friend like that!" This usually gets their attention.)

- Consider how you feel about yourself. Do you put yourself down all the time? If so, think of this as a habit that you can break.

- Try to treat yourself with the same admiration and compassion that you would give someone you care about. In other words, become your own best friend.

• • •

# CHAPTER 5

# Adult Children Raising Alcoholics

If they are determined to do so, children will experiment [with alcohol and other drugs] whether their parents want them to or not. The question is, what are *you* going to do?[1] —*Dr. Jan*

Odds are pretty good that when our older kids get into trouble, alcohol or other drugs are involved. Did we see it coming? Were we in denial? Every parent's biggest fear is that late-night knock on the door, that moment when we realize our child's teenage partying may have crossed the invisible line between experimentation and alcoholism or drug abuse. That fear can be even greater when that knock comes to the door of an ACoA parent who realizes they have now achieved a new unwelcome title and acronym. They are now an "adult child raising an alcoholic"—an ACRA. ACRAs often rationalize their children's behaviors, ignoring the warning signs that their children may be in trouble until there is a crisis. What may be urgent to a "normal" parent often won't even register on our ACoA radars.

## Stories from the Trenches

My friend Allie is the adult child of an alcoholic, and she is also a recovering alcoholic. A divorced mother of two, Allie has a seventeen-year-old son, Jeffrey, who may be developing a substance abuse problem. Allie represents so many of us ACoAs who struggle with our own addictions as we worry about our children's alcohol and drug use against the backdrop of our family history. We were raised in a home by one or more alcoholic parents; now our children live in such a home.

Allie and I were talking about our children over coffee recently. She said, "I remember the first time I suspected Jeffrey was drinking. I went snooping in his room and discovered three bottles of liquor in his closet. At first I was surprised, but the more I thought about it, the more I wasn't even sure how much I cared. I was twelve when I started drinking, and that seemed normal. So for my kid to start five years later even felt like a bit of an accomplishment. Then again, I wasn't raised in a normal household, so I can't trust my own judgment. I was tempted to slip into the old behavior, which was to close the closet door and ignore the incident."

I told her I would have done the same thing.

Allie went on to describe how instead she decided to act like a "good parent," which to her meant "going ballistic," dumping all three bottles down the drain, and reading Jeffrey the riot act when he got home. When I asked her how that went, she said, "He denied that the liquor belonged to him. He said that his buddy Steven took it from his parents' liquor cabinet, and that he hadn't touched a drop of it. And then he berated me for invading his privacy! I thought, 'Wow, he's a better liar than I was!' But I didn't trust that gut instinct that told me he was lying either. And then I felt remorseful about my accusations. So I called Steven's parents and told them that their son had taken three bottles of booze from their house and that I found them in my son's closet. Steven's parents confronted their son immediately, and he told them I was a liar and a drama queen. He told his parents that the stickers on the bottles would prove that they came from my ex-husband's local liquor store and that my son stole them from his father while he was there on a weekend visit. I was humiliated. Steven's parents never allowed him to come near my son or our home again. Every time I ran into his parents at a school function, they looked down their noses at me like I was a complete loser. A few months later, Jeffrey told me that Steven was suspended from school for smoking pot in the bathroom. I was secretly thrilled."

Can you identify with Allie's ambivalence and lack of self-confidence? She wanted to handle this situation the way a "normal" or "good" parent would, but because she grew up in the chaos of an alcoholic household, she had no frame of reference for what that means. If you're not sure how you feel about your kids' alcohol and drug use, you can't set boundaries for them or teach them your values—especially if you're unclear what those values are. When this happens, our children will probably make their own decisions without the maturity to do so—just like we did. But if we don't take a stand, our kids might think that it is okay with us if they experiment with alcohol or other drugs. We need to decide on the messages we want to send and then be consistent. If we set clear rules and boundaries about drinking and drugging and our kids breach our trust, they—not us—are responsible for their actions and the consequences of those actions. But it is our job to help them develop more mature consciences so they will be better able than we were to determine right from wrong. Here's how my mother explained it:

> The aspect of prevention can also be looked at largely in educational terms. Children need to be taught from a very early age to make decisions. That process is a learned one. They need to be taught to take responsibility for their behavior. They need to be taught to develop a value system so that they can think about their world and what it means to them. These

> tools and the education specific to the alcohol and drug use will help to afford youngsters a choice.[2] —Dr. Jan

Like Allie (and maybe like you), my upbringing has affected my ability to parent effectively in many ways—particularly when it comes to issues dealing with substance use and abuse. According to the National Council on Alcoholism and Drug Dependence, 17.6 million Americans suffer from alcohol abuse or dependence.[3] Every one of them is somebody's child.

Here's a recent "cyber chat" that I had with my twenty-two-year-old daughter, Rebecca (nicknamed Kiki), about her memory of my alcohol and drug "rules," which reveals just how ambiguous the messages we ACoAs send to our children can be.

> Me: What were my rules for you and your brother [Michael] regarding drug and alcohol use?
>
> Kiki: LOL [for readers who don't text, this is cyber shorthand for "laugh out loud"]. Not in the house. That's pretty much it.
>
> Me: And what was or is my opinion about my kids and drugs and alcohol?
>
> Kiki: Nothing concrete.
>
> Me: Did I ever give you the impression that I didn't care what you did?
>
> Kiki: No and yes.
>
> Me: Do you remember times that I found stuff in your room and went nuts?
>
> Kiki: Yup, but you never talked to me like a normal person about it. We never sat down and had a conversation. You didn't give limitations or curfew or

anything at all, so it made me feel like I could do whatever I wanted because there was no solid frame of thinking to fall back on.

Me: Is there anything I could've done to make you *not* drink or smoke pot, or would you have figured out how to do what you wanted no matter what?

Kiki: I think you could have been more open and honest about it as opposed to just getting upset and hysterical. This isn't a personal attack; I'm just being honest.

Me: Not a problem. But if you wanted to, which you did, would you have done it anyway?

Kiki: You didn't talk about it openly or voice your opinion, but I would have done what I wanted regardless because that's just me. But I'm sure I would have behaved *much* differently had you given limitations or at least stood your ground and voiced your opinions in a concrete way.

Me: Behaved much differently how?

Kiki: I would have behaved differently meaning had I had a curfew I wouldn't have been out all night or morning partying with idiots. There would have been less promiscuity because I would have been home. I would have respected you because I would have seen that you respected yourself and could stand your ground. Etc., etc.

Me: You wouldn't have snuck out of the house or told me to go f— myself if I had said no?

Kiki: Maybe, but I didn't respect you because you were so wishy-washy. You would just get upset about things. You never set any real limitations for any real reasons. There was never any open and honest discussion about anything. I know I didn't let you in, but that's because I felt like I couldn't trust you as a mother. Sorry.

Me: It's okay; I get it. So did the fact that I explained to you about alcoholism in the family have any impact on you?

Kiki: Yes. It made me understand why you handled our situations at home the way you did. I was empathetic to that fact, but still unforgiving . . . *then.*

Me: I mean, when I explained to you that alcoholism runs in the family and that it could happen to you . . . did that have any impact?

Kiki: No I didn't have addictive behavior. I was just depressed and rebellious.

Me: Do you have any addictive behaviors now?

Kiki: Nope . . .

Me: Last questions: What, if any, rules should parents have? Will kids find a way to do what they want to do no matter what? What advice would you give a parent so that they have the most chance of being listened to? Do you think kids should be allowed to party at home if they are underage? Should alcohol and pot be forbidden? Tell me any of your thoughts that you don't mind sharing, and I won't bother you anymore today! P.S.: When you have kids of your own, as they get older and you get older, I think you will understand me better—the way I understand my mom better. It's amazing what we learn when we realize we are standing in someone else's shoes.

Kiki: I bet. I'm kind of scared. LOL. But to answer your question, no, absolutely not—I don't think kids should be allowed to party at home. I think it's one thing for your parents to allow you to have a drink *with* them vs. having the entire high school breaking your furniture while inebriated. If they want to go party, give a curfew.

Me: You don't think they are safest at home?

Kiki: To have a freaking party? No, that's just dangerous and irresponsible.

Me: If you are going to drink and smoke, should a parent allow you to do it at home where you are safe or should you have to go somewhere else to do it even if you could be in harm's way?

Kiki: I think it would be okay to have a drink with your parent so there isn't so much taboo around the idea of drinking. I guess that's true for smoking too if the parent smokes with them.

Me: Nice try. Ha ha. So if I have rules and my kids blow me off, it's still better than giving them too much freedom? At least they know where I stand, and if they want to be little assholes, then that's on them not me, right? Just being general—not talking about you!

Kiki: Yes, that's on them, but it's your job to remain firm in your beliefs and discipline them as necessary . . . give them freedom but with limitations. For example—a curfew.

Me: Okay, but how else can you discipline except for taking away their vehicle if they have one?

Kiki: Grounding . . . but if they're over 18, kick them the f— out! LOL. Gotta go now. xoxoxo love you.

Me: You are adorable, and I can't wait until you have kids!

Kiki: I can! LOL.

If my mother were still with us, she could've shared her wisdom about me parenting her granddaughter as situations arose. But I have her words. It's a gift for me to find this piece of her advice all these years later and quite a surprise to find that grandmother and granddaughter think so much alike!

> It is important for children to have clearly defined limits. Give them parameters around which they can order their lives. It is the inconsistency that so disorients the children that they lose a sense of who they are. One cannot feel good about himself if he doesn't know what is going on from day to day. Children test limits just to know if you really mean them. If the rule is fair, it doesn't matter whether or not the child likes it. Few do. But that does not mean they will not be grateful for it and feel more secure because of it. One must feel secure if one is to improve his sense of himself. You can help with this feeling.[4] —Dr. Jan

### Action vs. Reaction

What impacted me the most about what my daughter said in our cyber chat was that my "wishy-washiness" made it impossible for her to trust me. Because I wasn't in charge, she didn't feel safe. That is a connection I would not have made on my own, and I am very grateful that she made me aware of this. Even though I can't go back and fix it now, the fact that we can reflect on it as part of our shared past is a gift. In thinking back and applying this idea to my own childhood, I can see how my mother's lack of taking charge had a traumatic effect on me, just as my lack of taking charge affected my daughter. Kiki and I both had to endure living situations that were toxic because of mothers (one of them *me*) who were so overwhelmed with what was happening to them personally that they could only *react* to what was happening beyond themselves—rather than act on their children's behalf. Though my mother recognized (and wrote about) what she observed and experienced in our own family and the families of so many other ACoAs, I still followed in her footsteps when it came to mothering my own children. Here's what Mom had to say about action vs. reaction:

> So, the first place we see victims of alcoholism is with the alcoholics themselves, so many of whom are from alcoholic families. The second place we see victims of alcoholism is with those who live with alcoholics. The alcoholic acts, the family reacts. The alcoholic is addicted to alcohol, the family is addicted to the alcoholic.[5]  —Dr. Jan

As many ACoAs do, Mom and I both stayed in unhealthy marriages too long instead of taking decisive actions to put a stop to what was going on. My children not only reacted to the alcoholism in our household but also to the chaos that comes from being raised by a codependent parent who doesn't take charge—just as I had done. As my mother observed, adult children of alcoholics often exhibit a generalized anxiety. But she said it wasn't always obvious where this came from.

I think it varies in terms of degree and influence of each parent. I have not been able to figure out in terms of the negative impact on kids if it is the chemical dependent or the codependent who is more damaging. We can't automatically decide that it's the alcoholic who does the most damage, and we can't automatically decide that it's the non-alcoholic who is most interested in getting their kids help. I have had many people really caught in their addiction who will say, "I may die from this, but please help my kids" and codependents who get so caught in this unhealthy system that they are unable to break free of it. So it depends on what help is available.[6] —*Dr. Jan*

As single mothers, my mother and I gave our children more freedom and less accountability for their actions than was in our children's best interest. Because we and our children had already been through so many crises, we thought we were giving our kids a break by letting them have a little fun for a change. We told ourselves that whatever drinking and drugs they were doing was a normal part of growing up. In reality, my daughter and I both acted out in large part in an effort to gain our parent's attention with a wish that they would put their foot down and take charge. The good news is that my unwelcome inheritance doesn't have to be my daughter's. We can learn and change the direction for the future.

Mom and I came to understand the relationship between our personal strength and our children's sense of safety and stability too late to change course at that time. I'm thankful, however, that Mom was able to share her newfound perspective with the ACoAs she taught, and I fervently hope that my children will benefit from these insights so their children will have clearer boundaries and the security that comes from having consistent and confident parents they can trust.

Trust means stability. It means that tomorrow's behavior will be similar to yesterday's. It means that you can count on things.[7]
—Dr. Jan

Establishing a secure environment in which trust can flourish requires taking an honest look at how our unwanted inheritance of addiction or our experience of growing up around addiction might be setting the tone of our home. Are we creating an atmosphere of anxiety and fear and instability without meaning to? Those of us with addictions know that these are the feelings that we tried to numb with our drug of choice—which means we must be especially diligent about encouraging our own children to find healthier ways to deal with their own emotions. This is why it's so important for us to focus on our recovery, so we can model the behavior that we want to pass down to our children.

When we do this self-examination, it's very important to view ourselves with the same compassion that we would show to a good friend who might be going through the same thing. It's also important to try to move beyond shame and blame. It's not our fault that alcoholism has taken root in our families and worked its way to our children. I wonder if my mother was speaking to herself as well as to ACoAs in the following passage:

> It is important for you to know that children of alcoholics are no more or less harmed emotionally than children living in any other kind of stressful situation. Alcoholism cannot claim exclusive rights to distressed children. The guilt that you carry because of your inability to provide an ideal home environment regardless of the circumstances is not going to do you a bit of good. It will not do your children a bit of good, either. All it will do is take energy away from the things that you could be doing to change the situation.[8]  —Dr. Jan

I've heard it said that guilt and shame are two sides of the same coin—that guilt is feeling bad about what you do, and shame is feeling bad about who you are. As ACoAs, most of us felt guilty that we could not stop our parent(s) from drinking, and now we may feel guilty because our children are showing signs that they have inherited an addiction disorder, despite our best efforts to prevent it. We may have enabled our kids to one degree or another, but would that have stopped this disease from taking hold of them? Maybe it would've just changed the story line a bit. Despite all of our knowledge and experience, our kids may develop addiction problems. We hope that our kids will be spared because of our experience, but sometimes it just doesn't work that way. Sometimes they still have to go through it themselves, just as we did. But our guilt about what they've inherited can prevent us from admitting that our children might have an addiction problem. In helping ACoAs come to terms with the fact that their child may have a problem with alcohol, my mother suggested that they ask themselves the following questions to understand what beliefs they may be holding, despite all of their knowledge and experience around alcoholism:

> Explore your own reality in regard to alcoholism. Are you judgmental? How do you stereotype? Do you consider alcoholism a moral weakness? Do you drink too much? Does someone you love? One of our biggest enemies in confronting alcoholism is the denial factor—how open and honest are you willing to be in terms of yourself? If you cannot be honest with yourself, can you expect your children to be honest with you? Take a look at what is in your way.[9]  —Dr. Jan

### We Are Not Alone

One thing I try to remember when I am going through a difficult time is that whatever my troubles, there are other people who have gone through what I'm experiencing and maybe worse. Knowing that we are not alone can reduce the isolation of living with addiction. Since Dr. Jan made the following statement over thirty years ago, the numbers of individuals affected by the disease of alcoholism continue to grow: We are not alone.

> The National Council on Alcoholism estimates that there are ten million alcoholics in this country. That is a conservative estimate at best. We do know that the numbers of alcoholics are increasing and that those who use the drug are doing so at a younger and younger age. [Note: This has proven to be especially true since this was written.] Many youngsters are brown bagging alcohol in the school. And the middle schools are no longer exempt from this problem. I found in my practice recently a woman who was alcohol dependent from the age of eight and drug dependent (by prescription) by the age of three. At least one out of every ten of you has or had a problem with alcohol. Alcoholism shows no social [or] economic bias and is not exclusive to any age group.[10] —Dr. Jan

We ACoAs who are raising children with potential or actual substance abuse issues have a unique challenge on our hands. Like all parents, we want the best for our children and we worry about them, especially when they are self-destructive in some way and not functioning well in their lives. Mom related to the helplessness that we parents feel especially when our children are adults, but she explained that our children are on their own journeys.

> I think frankly it is the hardest thing in the world to watch our children flounder and know that they have to flounder until they hurt enough so that they listen to what it was we told them in the beginning. And that's really the way it is with all children, and it's very, very hard to watch. But they have to

find their own way. I guess I say that to myself as much as to you.¹¹ —*Dr. Jan*

With the Serenity Prayer in mind, in chapter 6 we will look at our unwelcome inheritance in an effort to sort out what we can change for ourselves and our children and what we have no control over.

———————————— TAKEAWAY ————————————

**Together We Can Do What We Cannot Do Alone**

It has become second nature for many of us ACoAs to manage things by ourselves, so it can be very difficult to ask for and accept help when we need it. Addiction is known to be a disease of isolation—for both the addict and his or her family—and the antidote is love and support from others. Mom and I have both been so fortunate to have the encouragement and help of close friends who are experts in the field of addiction studies. I am especially grateful for the insights they continue to share about the intergenerational effects of addiction in families. One such friend is Tim Healy, an addictions specialist who has counseled addicts for more than twenty-five years.

When our children live under our roof with us, we can have rules that we enforce, and we can educate them to the best of our abilities in hopes that they will not become addicted to drugs or alcohol. However, it may happen that despite our best efforts, the disease will win. As Tim emphasizes, ultimately, recovery is a personal choice. Here's how Tim approaches working with alcoholics and drug addicts:

> There must be a desire for change. Many addicts do not believe there is a problem, despite overwhelming evidence. Present the addict with something they want to respond to or at least feel is possible for them

to achieve with help. Help them establish a support system, no matter how small. Addicts look for the flaw/angle/catch in any offer when first presented to them. Demonstrate to them that what you say is what you mean. Allow the person to make their own mistakes and, instead of walking away as they expect you to, stay and tell them it's going to be okay. As many times as it takes. This, by simple definition, pulls the consistency into place that makes it all work.[12]

Whether a child is at risk for addiction or is actively in its grasp, the perception that he or she is loved seems to make all the difference in terms of lowering that risk or aiding in the recovery process. Even from a purely clinical standpoint, we are told that the healing process is dependent on caring support from others. Dr. Jan's dearest friend, Professor V. G. Kay, has researched addiction since the 1980s, and she was instrumental—along with Dr. Jan—in igniting the movement for adult children of alcoholics. As she explains it, many ACoAs perpetuate the cycle of addiction in their families without intending to:

The cycle doesn't get completely broken because everyone is so wed to the disease model that they forget about the psychological component. It's a disease model with a psychological overlay, and if you are so focused on the disease and curing the disease, very often the psychological component still remains. Psychological treatment—whether it is Alcoholics Anonymous, therapy, or whatever—is the key to ongoing remission.[13]

Her words certainly ring true for me. It's hard to describe how valuable various Twelve Step groups have been to me and to my family. We discovered that the support and lifelong friendships that you can find there are unmatched, and the personal growth that you can experience can be life changing.

- If your child wants help because they have a problem with alcohol or other drugs, I suggest you get information about support groups in your area such as Alcoholics Anonymous (www.aa.org) that you can encourage your child to attend.

- If you feel your child (or anyone else that you love) has a problem and they don't want help, *you* can still get the support you need so that you can better cope with the impact their problem is having on you and your family. If this is the case, I encourage you to explore a resource such as Al-Anon (www.al-anon.org) to find a meeting near you that you can attend. Siblings of an addicted child may also benefit from groups like Alateen.

- Likewise, if you are concerned that you or a family member may be suffering from mental illness, which often goes hand in hand with substance abuse, contact an organization like NAMI (National Alliance on Mental Illness) through their website at www.nami.org.

The important thing to remember is help is out there. You don't have to walk this path alone.

• • •

# CHAPTER 6

# Breaking the Cycle

*Families want to maintain unhealthy systems sometimes, and it's not up to us to decide how other people should live their lives. Denial is largely when other people will not behave in the way we have decided is in their best interest. So we really need to look at what our goal is, whose needs we are serving, and whether we are being honest.[1]* —*Dr. Jan*

**W**hat does it mean to "break the cycle"? Is it really possible? We cannot change the fact that alcoholism is a disease that can be arrested but not cured. As described in chapter 2, addiction is a chronic brain disorder that can run in families, sometimes skipping generations. We can develop an addiction at any age. We don't have any more control over those facts than we have over how tall we are. But it is within our power to break *our* part of the cycle and be the catalyst for change and healing in our families. We can also educate our children about their unwelcome inheritance and obstruct the path of this disease to the best of our ability. Yes, it is within us to influence our loved ones in a positive way by becoming a "power of example," *but we have to be healthy ourselves.*

### Let It Begin with Me

Witnessing the havoc my father's alcoholism caused in our own home and learning all I did about the disease from my mother and Twelve Step meetings didn't stop me from having addiction problems of my own. In spite of this reality, I believe that knowing how dangerous alcohol and other drugs could be for me because of my family history helped keep my addiction problems from getting as bad as they could have been. Understanding the insidious nature of this disease also instilled in me the tools of recovery that I have always drawn on in life, even when using drugs and alcohol. I've also long understood that many of the serious problems I have had in adulthood are the direct result of growing up with alcoholism. However, even though I have always known where to go for help, I didn't always have that Serenity Prayer courage to change. As they often say at Twelve Step meetings, "Recovery Is a Process, Not an Event." I'm living proof of that, and I'm willing to bet that if you are reading this book, you are, too.

I got clean and sober in my twenties, and—except for a brief slip when my second marriage was breaking up—I didn't smoke or drink for more than twenty years. I believed that I was modeling sobriety for my children. And I was—and then again, I wasn't. While other parents kept a variety of liquor in their homes and openly drank in front of their kids, I did not. If someone brought me a bottle of wine as a gift, I'd probably re-gift it a year later. If someone brought a six-pack of beer over, it could sit in my fridge for several months until I poured it down the sink. One of my sons used to tease me for being such a square. He would say, "Mom, how can you let that beer sit there like that for so long and then pour it down the sink? *That's* alcohol abuse!" It felt good to show my kids that alcohol didn't have a place in our everyday lives. Some non-alcoholic ACoA parents drink in front of their kids because they believe that making a big deal out of alcohol might make drinking more desirable to their kids, who may think, "If my parents hate it, it must be good." We all have to handle this subject in a way that rings true for us.

I felt I was modeling sobriety through abstinence and house rules. And I feel that I have done a pretty good job imparting to my children the reality of their unwelcome inheritance in the sense that they've always known about our family history and the potential the disease of addiction has to grow in their lives because of their body chemistry. But because I continued to suffer for so many years with the low self-esteem that comes with being an ACoA and having the eating disorder I have struggled with for as long as I can remember, my kids were raised by an untreated ACoA and active addict. So in that sense, I was *not* the model of sobriety I congratulated myself on being. I was loving and supportive and was there with them every day of their lives. I was never violent or abusive. But I was in a constant state of depression, and I did not act on my children's behalf or on my own behalf as I should have. I was married twice, and though I knew my marriages were toxic and had to end, in the same way I knew my teenagers were drinking with their friends, I avoided taking a stand because I feared confrontation and was too overwhelmed to make decisions or take any healthy action. Instead of praying for "the courage to change the things I can," I prayed, "Please get me through this day." I made choices out of fear rather than faith, and I acted out of weakness rather than strength. It took me a long time to discover that this way of living out the past perpetuates the very behavior that we want to change.

*Let it begin with me.* I am the center of my family, and you are the center of yours. We are the bridge between the generations, and we are in a unique position to influence the future in such positive ways. In order to make a difference, we have to get healthy. Even if we have been in recovery for some time, we need to take it to the next level, whatever that means for each of us. I didn't want to face my addictions because I didn't want anyone to take them away from me. I couldn't imagine not having anything to relieve my anxiety and fear or to numb my pain. It took many years for me to learn that the only way to understand why I used substances was to stop using substances! I was also afraid of addressing certain barriers to my personal growth out of resistance to change. Finding the courage to change the things we can starts with ourselves. My sponsor tells me to ask my Higher Power for the willingness to change. She says that the whole point of recovery is to become the person we were intended to be. I would love nothing more than to encourage my children to do the same by my power of example. Now that's modeling sobriety.

If you had asked my mother how she went from the depths of despair to the *New York Times* Best Sellers list, she wouldn't have given you step-by-step instructions. She would have simply said to you, as she said to me one day during a mother-and-daughter chat,

> I took my energy back and I took my power back. And I put that energy and power into the things that were important to me.[2] —*Dr. Jan*

When we are feeling strong and have clarity and purpose, we can break *our* part of the cycle of addictive behavior that we perpetuate with our families. We can interact with our family members and others in a healthier and more positive way. And that is the very best place to begin to change the direction of our lives.

### Breaking the Cycle with Our Kids

> I remember my oldest son asking me if he could see a therapist, and I said, "Why can't I help?" And he said, "Because you are part of the problem." And it's true. We are. We have to be.[3] —*Dr. Jan*

When we are healthier in mind, body, and spirit, we respond differently to our children, family, and friends. We learn to address our concerns honestly and without fear instead of hiding in denial. We learn to say what we need to say and do what we need to do.

Remember my friend Jackie from chapter 3? As I mentioned, her grandparents were alcoholics and her parents were both ACoAs who did not drink, yet she became an alcoholic. Her son became addicted to heroin when he was seventeen years old, and because Jackie was drunk much of the time, she did not realize that her son was in danger. Jackie was charged with four DWIs and had to serve time in jail before she accepted the fact that she was an alcoholic. When she had a year or two of sobriety under her belt, she became able to face the fact that her son was addicted to heroin. She was terrified and knew that she couldn't help him if she wasn't sober. She hasn't had a drink since. Now, three years sober and still in AA, Jackie is healthier than she has ever been before and has become part of the solution instead of part of the problem. She is a stronger mother than she has ever been. Using the tools that she has learned in recovery as well as the lessons she gained from her life experience, she has stopped enabling her son's heroin abuse and has gotten him into treatment.

Around midnight on the night things began to change for her son, Jackie called me and said, "Danny says he's ready to go to detox. What should I do?" Jackie was no longer allowed to drive because of her DWI charges, so I drove over to her house to pick them up and take them to the nearest rehab facility. We both knew that if we let this moment pass, Danny might change his mind, and the opportunity to get him help could be lost indefinitely. We called the nearest inpatient rehab and asked if we could bring him over right away. They wanted us to wait until the next day, but we worried that, by then, Danny would want to use again to ward off his withdrawal symptoms, and our opportunity could be lost.

We arrived at the detox unit at approximately two in the morning and brought Danny inside. The manager on duty was at first furious by Jackie's audacity—bringing her son there in the middle of the night when they told her not to come until the next day. But within a minute or two, this same manager admitted that this young man was lucky that his mom knew she had to "strike while the iron was hot." Jackie said she also knew that when Danny returned home after treatment, he would need her more than ever.

> Before a child leaves treatment, we need to be assured that there is one person in that child's life whom they can run to who will be there for them. If we don't do that, we're just perpetuating the cycle. This person might be a sponsor, if it can't be a parent. That seems to be what makes the critical difference.[4] —Dr. Jan

Danny completed detox and a thirty-day inpatient treatment program. Since returning home six months ago, he has not used heroin, although Jackie suspects that he has used alcohol and marijuana. Even if he has slipped, it does not mean that the time in treatment was a waste. Danny knows there is help available for him if he wants it, and whatever he learned in those thirty days will, we hope, take hold when he is ready. In the meantime, his mother has become the role model she always wanted to be. Danny knows that his mother is an active member of AA, and he can't help but notice her new, healthy behavior. Jackie has made it clear through her words and actions that drug and alcohol use are not allowed in her home under any circumstances, and that her son can finally trust that she will be there for him every step of the way.

Jackie is encouraged that she was able to be proactive instead of living in denial. She admits that had she not been in recovery, she would not have been able to help her son that night. She is grateful that he wanted help and came to her, and she was able to step up with strength and leadership. The lines of communication are open between her and Danny. Jackie accepts that she cannot control whether Danny uses or recovers. But there are new boundaries in place that serve to make her home a clean, sober, and stable home.

It is very common for us to want to make our loved ones stop drinking or using drugs because it is clear to *us* that they have a problem and *we* are ready for them to recover. Jackie has opened a pathway for her son to travel further down at any time *he* chooses. She knows that participation in his own recovery has to come from him. Dr. Jan would agree with Jackie that this is the only way toward long-lasting recovery.

> The first question that I invariably hear from people is "How do I get my mother, wife, husband, sister, brother, son, daughter to stop drinking when they don't think they have a problem?" You can't. Well, that's not quite true. You can always lock them up! That way, you make them stop it for a while; however, when you lock them up, be sure to remove not only the alcohol. You must also remove the mouthwash, aftershave lotion, toothpaste, and cough syrup. Once you decide to release them, they may go back to drinking again. If someone really gives up drinking, they do it because *they* want to.[5] —Dr. Jan

## Trusting Our Instincts

As ACoAs, we could not effect the changes we wanted in our own lives until we wanted to and were willing to. In the past, we have usually not trusted our own instincts or our own judgment. We have second-guessed our perceptions and made excuses for the unacceptable behavior of others in order to avoid confrontation. When we come from a place of strength with the goal of breaking the cycle of addiction in our families, we think differently. As Dr. Jan encouraged, we begin to trust ourselves and our viewpoints because our life experience has taught us well.

> Another question I hear a whole lot is "I have a child who has a drinking problem. I don't know whether he is an alcoholic or not, but I'm concerned about it. What should I do?" Usually I find that if someone is concerned about their child's drinking, the response is never "Don't worry about it." Usually there's a reason to worry about it.[6] —Dr. Jan

We've talked about how we ACoAs tend to deny problems until the point of crisis. We fall into the addictive thinking that tells us, "The next time it happens, I'll say something or do something. This is the last time I will allow this! Tomorrow will be different." We act this way because we are afraid or have no idea what to do. Dealing with an issue in the moment that it is happening is new behavior for many of us, and it takes practice.

One night when my daughter was a teenager, she wanted to spend the night at a friend's house. Since the first time I met this friend, my gut told me that she was trouble, and I didn't trust her. I told my daughter about my concern, and she immediately pointed out that my opinion was baseless because nothing bad had ever happened. She was understandably upset at me for judging her friend so harshly when I'd had no reason to. Against my better judgment, I reluctantly gave in and allowed her to go.

During the night, my daughter and her friend snuck out of the house and met up with some other kids. They hung out at a local park and drank beer until the police found them and drove them home. The bad news was I didn't know that I could just refuse to allow the sleepover simply because I felt uncomfortable with the idea. I didn't know that as a parent I was (and am) allowed to say "No" without justifying my reasons. It took the police at my door to validate my concerns. The good news was that I felt empowered enough to take (or rather, drag) my daughter to a clinic for a substance abuse evaluation, and it was determined that she was not abusing alcohol or drugs. (Whew!)

Opinions vary as to how to determine who is an alcoholic. Professionals use varying assessment tools. Support groups offer self-assessment tools. And in chapter 2 of this book, I list the eleven criteria the American Psychiatric Association uses to diagnose a substance use disorder. Dr. Jan had a simple way of looking at this question.

> An alcoholic is someone whose alcohol use is causing a problem in any area of their life. Alcoholism is a disease that you may have or you may develop, so it's not too relevant in this case as to whether or not someone really is an alcoholic. It has to do with whether or not they believe that alcohol is getting in their way of being all that they can be.[7] —Dr. Jan

At that very first ACoA meeting my mom held in our house, she pointed out that we aren't as powerless as we might think. As she said, we can often help just by being there when a loved one with an addiction disorder is ready to get help, as she demonstrated in this conversation at the first ACoA group meeting:

> *Man:* I have a stepdaughter whose father's parents were alcoholics. Both of them. And it's real hard for her to see the relationship between her and her father and how the issues she struggles with are related to issues that were present in past generations. My wife doesn't think there is anything we can do about that.
>
> *Dr. Jan:* How is your stepdaughter doing? How old is she?
>
> *Man:* She's twenty-two years old.
>
> *Dr. Jan:* She's twenty-two years old and how is she operating in her life?
>
> *Man:* In many ways, not very effectively. She's still living at home, she goes out drinking several times a week, she is unemployed, has trouble with males—several things aren't working well for her.
>
> *Dr. Jan:* And you can't control any of it. But that's the struggle. And when she gets into difficulty in the here and now, she will address it. What I do with my own children is I have a therapist available for them at a minute's notice. [She laughed when she said this.] So when the time comes, I am ready. So what I suggest to you is have the resources in place for when she asks for help, and respect her enough to let her have her struggle right now.[8]

The parents in this example had decided that they wanted their daughter to continue to live at home with them. My mom did not challenge that decision, but I know many parents who have spent many years in Twelve Step recovery groups who would. Despite how painful it was, some of these parents turned their children away when they had nowhere else to go because they knew that taking them in would keep them from reaching rock bottom. They know that alcoholism is a disease that is "cunning, baffling, and powerful," to use the Big Book description, and that the more we protect our kids, the longer it can take for them to get the help they need, and the harder they might fall.

My friend Kevin says that when he was twenty-four years old, his drinking and drug use began to take a toll on his family, and his parents threw him out. He lived out of his car for six months, and every day he called his father and begged him to let him come home. Finally, his father said, "You can come home if you stay clean and sober and get into treatment. If you mess up one time, you're out and you're not coming back." Kevin just celebrated six years clean and sober. When he shares his story of substance abuse and recovery, he says that kicking him out of the house was the best thing his parents could have done for him. His parents will tell you that they hated themselves and were terrified when they told Kevin to pack his stuff and leave. Looking back, they realize that it was the right decision, and the hardest thing they ever had to do.

It is difficult not to be codependent with our kids. Our parental instinct is to protect them from harm and suffering. But if we truly believe they inherited this disease, and we shield them from the reality of what they've inherited, we become part of the problem. It may seem counterintuitive, but if we overprotect our children, we might be denying our son or daughter their life lessons and the journey that was meant to be for them. We are denying them the opportunities to grow through their hardships, as we have grown through ours. When I think of it this way, I realize that despite it all, I turned out to be a pretty good person.

My friends who are further along than me in their recovery (and in their parenting) tell me that they think their efforts to "protect" their children were selfish because it made *them* (not their children) feel better and helped *them* (not their children) sleep better at night. They say this without judging themselves, but with compassion for themselves and the recognition that this is excruciatingly painful for all of us as parents. This perspective gives us a different lens through which to view this problem, helping us realize that our efforts to "fix" everything can enable the disease of addiction to progress.

A few years ago, my son Mike had a problem that I tried to "fix." He became frustrated with me for what I thought was helping and what he considered to be my constant interference. He said, "Mom, why are you always trying to fix everything? You can't fix this; it's just the way it is!" I considered that for a moment and realized that he was absolutely right. I was powerless to fix anybody but myself. Smiling, I replied, "Son, don't you realize my way is better?" In the end, Mike worked it out his own way and felt like more of an adult because I gave him his space. And the biggest surprise of all? I was so relieved to let go of the problem. *His* problem. I'm not saying don't listen to your kids. Listening to them with an open heart and mind is one of the greatest gifts you can give them, and having them trust you enough to share their concerns is one of the greatest gifts they can give you. I'm just suggesting that you—that we all—practice listening without rushing to judgment or being too eager to fix whatever problems our children are sharing with us. When they want our advice, they'll let us know.

Here's another way to look at this same problem in a less emotional context: My son Josh is in middle school. His homework takes a lot of time, and he loves it when I help him. He wants to give me words to look up, or typing to do, and sometimes he reels me right in—hook, line, and sinker. He knows that I'm tired after a long day at work and that I don't want to spend the whole night supervising him doing his homework. He also knows that I hate to see him frustrated or upset. So he looks at it as a team effort and tries to divvy up the work between us. I am finally becoming wise in my old age and realizing that when I do his work, he doesn't learn all he could be learning—except perhaps the art of parent manipulation. If I make it easier for him, he doesn't have to put in the same effort as he would otherwise. He doesn't take ownership for his work, and he has more expectations of me than are appropriate. So now when he asks me to help him, I say, "Josh, I already did my sixth-grade homework, and you can do yours, too!" Doing it himself gives him a sense of accomplishment, and he remembers what he learns.

So when we want to rush in and do the homework for our kids (or solve their other problems), let's take a breath, stop ourselves, and try to remember—the lessons they are learning will mean more if they work through a problem and arrive at a solution on their own. In the meantime, we can work on our own growth and self-care—something my mother consistently encouraged ACoAs to do because many of us tend to care for others to the point of neglecting ourselves.

> It has been my experience that the clients I see who come from alcoholic homes need to be taught that their primary responsibility is to themselves.[9] —Dr. Jan

I admire my recovering friends more than words can say. They have an inner strength and deep wisdom that I hope to have one day. They teach me that I need to take care of myself in the midst of chaos, and that there's no such thing as perfect parenting. We have to do what is right for us, and we have to be able to live with our decisions. One size does not fit all. If you know in your heart that it's time to let your son sit in jail instead of bailing him out again, do it. If you decide to pay your daughter's legal fees one more time, do that. Maybe you are uncomfortable giving your child money that they may spend on alcohol and drugs, but you like the idea of purchasing their necessities yourself, so you do that. If it would be good for you, tell your kids what you see and how it makes you feel so they realize that what they are doing affects you, too: "I know I can't stop you from drinking, but every time you walk out the door, I feel terrified that something will happen to you." If you need outside support, go to Al-Anon or to a person with whom you are comfortable sharing confidences. Take care of yourself! This too shall pass. But you'll get through it more easily if you practice good self-care and have the right kind of support.

As a probation officer, I specialized in supervising high-risk youth who were under eighteen years old. In Juvenile Justice, "high risk" means "likely to end up incarcerated" (my definition), and it was my job to make sure that this didn't happen—at least not on my watch. On a daily basis, per my supervisor, I had to direct parents to call the police on their children if they did not know where they were, or I had to discuss with them the option of pressing charges against their son or daughter if something their children did at home constituted a crime. What a fraud I felt like, knowing that I would never call the police on my kids in a million years!

In most every case, the youth in question had been abandoned by at least one parent, a factor that increased risk levels many times over if he or she tested positive for drugs and admitted to some amount of alcohol use. In these situations, my first action would be to find that absent parent and hold them accountable to assist their child in meeting their "conditions of probation," whether it be driving them to school or work, making sure they completed their community service, or making sure they attended outpatient treatment. I tried to get them to do something, anything, for and with their children. *Even if the parent openly resented the obligation in front of the child,* the positive impact this had on the youth's behavior was incredible—whereas they felt irrelevant in the past, they now perceived that their parent loved them and that they were important. I had never seen anything but a scowl on one particular boy's face, but on the days he came walking down the hall to my office with his dad, he beamed with pride. This made all of the difference in the world. I can't say for sure that such cases closed successfully solely for this reason, but it sure did seem like it to me. Dr. Jan once explained that how the parent really feels doesn't matter as long as the child believes that they are loved.

> The perceived love of the child by the parent is even more critical than the actual love. [M.] Scott Peck wrote about how love is behavior—the difference between kids who get into drugs and those who don't has to do with this perceived love. It does not necessarily have to be the parent, but somebody the child connects to in a meaningful kind of a way.[10] —*Dr. Jan*

Every kid is one loving adult away from a better life. Know that you *do* make a difference. Set clear boundaries and be consistent. Tell your kids you will always love them no matter what. Remember that you are affected by their behavior, too, and that it is totally normal to feel sad, angry, fearful, confused, guilty, ashamed, and every other emotion under the sun—and that you may even resent your kids for putting you through such a hard time. Remember what my best friend, Tommy, told me before he died: "Feelings Aren't Facts."

Remember that it is not your fault, but it *is* your responsibility to do what you can. The hardest thing is to make a decision and stick to it. Get the support you need. And never, ever, ever give up on yourself!

--- TAKEAWAY ---

**Parenting Can Be Messy**

Take the time to think through your feelings and opinions on this subject. Read Dr. Jan's books *Adult Children of Alcoholics* and *Healthy Parenting*. Speak to parents you trust and respect who have kids you genuinely like. Go to Al-Anon and hear about how other parents and loved ones approach parenting issues. If you do nothing else, tell your kids about the disease of addiction and how alcoholism or drug addiction runs in your family. Let them know that the chances of becoming alcoholics are greater for them, and that you are doing what you can to protect them.

Every situation is unique, and there are no perfect answers that fit every case. We need to take into account what we believe is the right approach and the temperaments of our children. Parenting can be messy and difficult, but we only get one chance to raise our kids and to keep them safe from themselves and the rest of the world.

There is always much to learn, but here are some positive things that ACoA parents generally have in common that give us a foundation on which to build healthy change:

1. We love our children.
2. We want them to be happy, healthy, and successful in their lives.
3. We do the best we can with what we have.
4. We are better parents than we give ourselves credit for.

5. We are ready to do better and to start wherever we may be on our own path of recovery and healthy parenting.

Even if you feel torn or confused about how you should think or feel or act, here are some parenting tips to keep in mind as you continue to sort out your own personal issues:

- When you talk to your kids about their genetic predisposition toward alcoholism and about your concerns for their health and safety, speak to them as if they are adults. Tell them that you love them and that you worry about them. Don't lecture or talk down to them. Listen with respect to what they have to say, even if they are telling you that you're overreacting and that you don't know what you're talking about. Tell them that it's your job to take care of them and protect them, and if they get angry with you or embarrassed by you, that's a risk you're willing to take. Let them know that if they are ever in a bad situation or stranded or have a vehicle and they have been drinking, that you are always there to come and get them. Try not to yell at them until the next day.

- Get to know your children's friends and their parents. Encourage your kids to invite their friends over to your home or offer to provide transportation. You'll create opportunities to get to know which friendships to encourage, whom to restrict their contact with, and whom to keep an eye on. Keep an ongoing and up-to-date list of the phone numbers of your children's friends so you can always find your kid. Offer your phone number to your children's friends as an emergency number to keep in their phones. Stay in the loop however you can!

- Underage drinking is illegal and dangerous. Don't allow it in your home, and don't let your underage kids go anywhere you suspect there may be alcohol. Tell them it's against the law and you want them safe. Expect them to get ticked off at you for "ruining their lives," and remind yourself that if your kids "hate" you for protecting them, you're doing a good job!

- Drinking and driving is deadly and should be prevented at all costs. If you have concerns about your children's drinking or other substance abuse, don't allow them to get their driver's license until they are ready. You might want to tie their behavior to driving privileges. Make sure to have your own set of keys to whatever car your son or daughter drives so you can remove it from the premises if necessary to keep them from using it, or so you can confiscate it if necessary.

- Try not to let them "see you sweat"! You can let them know when something is a difficult subject for both of you, but try to be strong and firm and loving at the same time. Try not to let your insecurity show through so that they think you can be manipulated. If you need to have a meltdown, hold yourself together until you have a private moment to sneak off to the bathroom for a quick cry, or to call your spouse or significant other or a friend.

- Know that even the best-laid plans sometimes fall apart and that we can't control everything our children do. Even those "perfect" parents have kids who are out of control, so don't blame yourself when things don't go according to your wishes. Your kids may test your authority and get drunk every now and again, but it doesn't have to be the end of the world. They may develop full-blown alcoholism and get into trouble despite all of your best efforts. Take it one day at a time and carry on.

- Trust your instincts! If you think there is a problem, there probably is. You've already lived through this, so you know what you are seeing. Let your past work for you—and for your children.

* * *

# CHAPTER 7

# Breaking the Cycle of Anger and Resentment

When one becomes aware of one's history, the first thing that usually happens is a sense of relief that you're not alone or crazy. After the initial relief, the pain can begin to surface. That pain is very big and real and overwhelming, but we can't deny it. Then anger can surface and must be addressed. It is not unusual for all the anger that has been bottled up over those years to bubble up to the surface, and folks get fearful of their own rage. All of the grief and loss. The awareness of what these stages are will help people not be frightened when they feel it.[1] —*Dr. Jan*

When I got that postcard from my father that I described in an earlier chapter—the one that said, "I'm sorry you feel that way," in response to my rage-filled fourteen-page letter about how he ruined my life—I felt rejected, shocked, and angry. I'd stare at it constantly, trying to understand what it meant and how I felt inside. It seemed like he didn't care about what I had gone through—that he thought I was overreacting, that he had no regrets of the past. I assumed that what *I* wrote to him didn't affect him at all. I wasn't ready to consider his point of view or his side of the story, or that he might not remember what I remembered, or that my letter hurt him terribly. As my mother explained regarding this common phenomenon among ACoAs, I had decided what my father was thinking because I didn't know how to speak to him.

> Another part of this educational process has to do with the fact that we have probably never really spoken honestly to each other. We guess how the other person is feeling and how we are supposed to feel and respond. [If you] ask an ACoA how they are feeling . . . they will probably look to you to see how they think *you* would feel. If you grew up in this system, it's likely that you did not get to ask questions and get them answered. You probably make assumptions about how others are feeling and responding and, of course, feel that if anyone is unhappy or angry, it's probably because of something you did. The whole notion of checking things out to find out what is really going on is an idea that is foreign to those living in a chemically dependent system. I find myself asking ACoAs, "Did you ask? Did you find out what was really going on?" Most often I find that they made assumptions based on the person's behavior.[2]  —*Dr. Jan*

For some reason, my feelings toward my father eventually began to shift. It was therapeutic for me to write that letter and to know that he had read it. It released the hurt and anger that had lived inside of me since my youth. Looking back now, it makes me sad to see that the only way I knew how to express myself was through rage and with the wish of hurting my father so that he could "have a taste of his own medicine." But that is how it happened. Now, all these years later, when I think of his postcard, his words sound like the truth. Surely, he was sorry that I felt that much hate and resentment toward him and that I felt he had ruined my life. The anger that I'd held for so long began to dissipate when I was a young adult. But it was replaced with sadness and emptiness. Dad had been sober for fourteen years at that time, and although he wasn't the father I wanted him to be, he certainly was not the father of my childhood whom I wrote that letter to.

Feelings of revenge or desire to punish are not unusual for ACoAs. Marie's daughter has these similar feelings toward her mother, and it is painful for both of them.

### Marie's Story

My friend Marie is seventy-eight years old and has been sober in AA for twenty-two years. She has one child, a daughter who is fifty years old, whom we will call Kim. Marie lives in New York City, and Kim moved to California shortly after her mother stopped drinking. Marie says that their relationship is horrible and that they have only seen each other a few times over the past two decades. Each time they get together, whether it's in person or over the phone, the visit deteriorates into an argument, and years go by before they get together again. Marie feels that everything she says makes her daughter angry, and it is very difficult for her to make even casual conversation without saying something wrong. Their phone calls are fewer and farther between. As the years go by, Marie continues to lose the hope of ever having a loving mother-daughter relationship with Kim in this lifetime, and she is heartbroken.

Marie knows that her daughter is still furious with her over all the things that happened when she was drinking. Marie is not the adult child of an alcoholic and so doesn't fully understand her daughter's point of view or what Kim went through as a child. Marie has no idea how to respond when her daughter brings up the past, except to say that she is sorry and that she wishes she could take it all back.

Knowing that she could not change the past, Marie has

worked to become a more attentive and dependable person through the years. By remaining committed to her recovery on a daily basis, she continues to do what Twelve Step groups would call "living" amends. This effort has been totally lost on Kim. When Marie told Kim she was going to her regular support group meeting to celebrate her twentieth year of sobriety, Kim couldn't care less. She muttered something that sounded like, "Good for you, Mom. Way to keep the spotlight on yourself."

Marie described a few times that her daughter lashed out at her, bringing up incidents from her childhood. She was caught off guard and couldn't find any words except for "I'm sorry." Kim told her mother that it felt good to get that hurt off of her chest and that her mother deserved it.

I hope Kim will come to have a change of heart, as I did when I was still in college. It was a warm spring day on campus, and graduation was right around the corner. I was sitting in my living room looking out the window, contemplating that baffling postcard once again. And just like that, it dawned on me that my father was not capable of meeting my needs. He wasn't evil or insensitive. He simply could not give me what I needed because he did not have it to give. I wanted him to be someone he was not. In this moment of clarity, I saw his limitations and began to understand them. I felt like I had truly been granted the serenity to accept that Dad, like me, was a product of his troubled upbringing, and that was one of the things I could not change.

### Letting Go of Expectations

Have you ever heard the saying "Expectations are premeditated resentments"? When we let go of our expectations of others or the hope that the other person will change, it lessens the tendency to be continually disappointed or angry. We can use the opportunity to take better care of ourselves by making whatever adjustments are needed for us to feel comfortable in the relationship. We can decide what our boundaries will be and how we will handle problems when they arise.

In reflecting on my father's upbringing, it occurred to me that if I had no warm memories of my grandparents (his parents), maybe he didn't either. I don't even recall a hug or a smile from either of my paternal grandparents. I remember how bitter my grandmother was and how quiet my grandfather was. They weren't warm and fuzzy people, and I wondered whether my dad ever felt loved by them. Maybe one of the reasons he drank was to numb the pain of feeling unloved. I became compassionate toward my father as a human being with a story of his own. Many years of education about alcoholism taught me that my father had a disease, and knowing that made me feel better because I knew his alcoholism wasn't my fault. Yet in spite of knowing this, I had always thought of the disease in terms of how it affected *my* life, never in terms of how it affected *his* life. Finally—almost without consciously realizing it—I made a decision to leave the "door of reconciliation" open a crack just to see what would happen.

Do you have a parent or sibling or other loved one you no longer speak to? Perhaps there was some sort of falling out, and you haven't spoken with them since. When you stop to think about this person, do you become emotional and exasperated all over again? It might be worth considering leaving that door open to the possibility of reconciliation. Dr. Jan says that we can look to ourselves to know whether this is a good idea.

One of the greatest gifts that adult children have is that you usually develop this gut instinct . . . which you don't trust . . . but you really can. You can use it for yourselves. It's marvelous.[3] —Dr. Jan

The next several years were a whirlwind. I graduated from college and, after a month at home with Mom, found myself clean and sober and bored and lonely. As usual, during the summer I worked at her institute, organizing and managing the educational programs and support groups and running our summer camp for ACoAs. But I had no social life, and I was tired of working in the family business. I applied to and was accepted into a graduate program in art therapy at New York University and abruptly moved into Manhattan to enjoy the rest of the summer before classes started. My life was a clean slate in this new place, and I had no schedule and no commitments.

Quickly, I became an example of addictive behavior in sobriety. Because I was a night owl, I started my day at the "Midnight Madness" Twelve Step meeting in Times Square, which met every night. There, I met an amazing group of new friends and even reunited with a few of my college buddies who were getting sober, too. After the meeting, we'd go to a nearby diner, and then I would walk alone back to my apartment at three in the morning or so. To be a young woman, alone, walking from Times Square to the Upper West Side of New York City at that hour was very high-risk behavior. I didn't see it that way, though. It was exciting and made me feel like I had a life of my own. My adrenaline pumped just like it did in my household as a child, just as it did when I was drinking and getting high.

The semester started, and within the first month I was miserable. Except for the studio art classes, I hated every minute of school and the program I was in, so I couldn't retain anything that I read or heard in class. The idea of becoming a therapist like my mother made me feel sick and anxious. I thought I knew who I was and what I wanted, and now I was having an identity crisis. I went to the head of the department and said, "I don't want to *be* a therapist. I *need* a therapist. Could you please give me a referral?"

At our first meeting, the psychiatrist to whom I was referred told me that I was so defensive she would not see me less than three times a week. She said any less would be like starting over at every visit, and she didn't care to waste her time that way. So I agreed, and in a short time it felt like I was being boiled alive. I wanted to rant and rave about my father, the alcoholic whom I was convinced was the root cause of all of my problems. She didn't care to hear it. She believed that I was repressing incredibly intense rage at my mother for not putting an end to what went on at home when I was a child. She also said that, unconsciously, I believed that in order to be loyal to my mother, I had to align with her and resent my father the way she did. The therapist asked why I went to recovery meetings for alcoholics when I clearly had an eating disorder. A few months later, when I got engaged, she questioned my timing and my choice of a husband. As a way to run from this uncomfortable introspection, I told her that three visits each week cost more than I could afford, and I terminated therapy. I wasn't ready to look at any of this stuff, although her words stewed in my brain for years. Mom actually talked about how ACoAs often flee treatment when they come up against feelings that scare them. She said they usually show their pain upon entering therapy, but their anger is buried. When it is uncovered, they want to (and often do) run away because they are hearing things they don't want to hear.

I share these experiences and feelings because I suspect they parallel many of yours, and I'm hopeful that sharing them will somehow normalize them for you. We are not alone. I am living proof of how powerful the grip of addiction is when it infects a family system. I acted and reacted in the "ACoA way" even though my mother was a leading authority on ACoA treatment and prevention. As my mother pointed out in the quote that leads into this chapter, my rage bubbled to the surface when I came face to face with it, and it scared the hell out of me.

Although I could not admit it for many years, the psychiatrist I saw when I was in college was right. As much as I always loved and cherished my mother, I was angry with her for taking so long to stop what was going on at home when I was a child. I was angry that she didn't respond to my obvious cries for help when I was acting out as a teenager. I had directed all of my wrath and blame toward my father for all those years, and it was enormously difficult to realize I harbored some of the same feelings toward my mother—the non-alcoholic in the family. Like alcoholism and other drug addictions, untended anger can also weave a tangled web that envelops generations. Although Mom connected the dots between an ACoA's delinquent behavior and their anger, I did not benefit from those insights until much later in my life.

> We [therapists] are fortunate with the children of alcoholics who act out, because when these kids act out, we gain the opportunity to address their rage. As clinicians, we must be mindful of this so that we do not miss out on this opportunity.[4] —Dr. Jan

As I mentioned early on in this book, even as a young adult, I admired and respected Mom's hard work and was thrilled beyond words at her success. What an incredible role model! At the same time, though, I was angry that ACoAs all over the world were getting the help that I so desperately needed. So many of the best professionals in the field at that time were Mom's colleagues, trainees, or employees. There seemed to be no one left with whom I could have a private therapeutic relationship. I was consumed with guilt and self-loathing for resenting my mother, whom I loved so much, who had been through hell and back, and who was able to use her experience to help so many people.

I'd given up alcohol, drugs, and cigarettes, so the only drug I had left to numb out with was sugar. The pounds starting piling on, one pint of ice cream at a time. Although Mom understood how ACoAs could carry so many conflicting feelings in their hearts at the same time, I never talked to her about *my* mixed-up feelings toward her. It was easier to swallow them with sugar or turn them into anger toward my alcoholic father. I loved my mother, so I couldn't be angry with her—which is typical ACoA "logic." As the following passage shows, she understood this perfectly when it came to other ACoAs, but somehow neither of us applied it to me or my suppressed feelings. Maybe she was afraid of going there, too.

> So many of us are afraid of our own anger. We're taught that anger is bad, and you're not supposed to be angry because anger is rage. That is one of the things that causes people to develop drug and alcohol problems. They are so afraid of losing control of their anger that they use substances to maintain control. Most ACoAs learned as children that it never does any good to express anger. It never made anything better. Somehow there is the message "If I love you, I can't be angry at you, and if you love me, you can't be angry at me, so if we love each other, we can't express any angry feelings." So anger gets pushed down until it becomes unmanageable. Most ACoAs go right from anger to rage without ever recognizing it—causing themselves a lot of problems. Many turn this anger on themselves and become suicidal. Fear of anger. Tight, tight control. What will happen if I lose control? When anger finally does get expressed, it often gets expressed in terms of rage, and rage invariably boomerangs.[5] —Dr. Jan

With the emotional grad school and psychiatrist fiascos neatly tucked away in the past, I felt better. It had been my dream to live and work in Manhattan. I loved the fast pace of the city and the eclectic people there. When I landed a dream job at the *Village Voice* newspaper in Greenwich Village, writers and artists were all around me. Going to work was like going to a party every day, all the way down to the smell of pot smoke coming from the next department. My colleagues and supervisors were all familiar with my mother's books, and when Mom appeared on *Oprah* in 1989, my boss hooked up a television so everyone could watch. What a thrill to watch Oprah introduce my mom as the woman who "began the Adult Children of Alcoholics movement—now six million strong— with her landmark book."

I was proud that my family's experience was helping others heal their lives in numbers that were astonishing. Excited, Mom and I continued to discuss what to offer at Mom's institute to help ACoAs further their recovery in all of the different areas of life. I became more excited about the future and less regretful of the past. It was the happiest time of my life so far.

That same year, my mother's brother, who was younger than her, died of a rare adrenal cancer, only in his forties. We were all heartbroken, and Mom was devastated. We were in Israel visiting his grave for the first time, and she collapsed in the cemetery. We all assumed that she fainted from the shock of reality that her brother was gone. When we arrived home, Mom saw her doctor and mentioned to him what had happened in the cemetery. He ran tests and called her and said, "Pack your bag, because you are going to the hospital. I will call you when they have a bed ready." A few days later, she called me and said, "I have something important to tell you." After a long pause, she said, "It's malignant." The room started to spin and then snapped back into focus when she ordered me to "stop hyperventilating."

At the most exciting time of her life and at the height of her career, after losing both of her parents and her only brother in a few years' time, my mother was diagnosed with a rare tumor that, at that time, only seventy people in the world had ever developed. Her first surgery required three separate teams of surgeons, twenty-two in all, and they were not confident that she could survive the operation that was supposed to save her life. Mom was determined to live, though, saying over and over, "It's not my time. I have too much to do." The outpouring of support and love from ACoAs all over the world and from friends, family, and colleagues was astounding and gave her the will to live. We were inspired to learn how much she was loved by the people she was most devoted to—ACoAs like you and me. In 1993, she wrote that "the power of the prayer and love and good wishes that had poured in from all over the world had made their energy felt" and that "the love of friends had offered a life-giving force" (Dr. Jan's personal handwritten notes, undated).

It took almost a year for Mom to recover from that first surgery, and it was such a gift when she walked me down the aisle at my wedding. Thankfully, she knew and loved her first two grandchildren before the cancer recurred for the third time and ultimately took her life on June 9, 1994. Twenty years later, we still receive condolences from ACoAs who have just discovered Mom's work, only to find out that she is no longer with us. What an incredible legacy she has left for us all to share.

I wrote the following piece about Mom's funeral many years later in an effort to describe my profound grief and also to try to capture the miracle I experienced at my mother's burial.

Horrified and sobbing, I stared down into the cold, empty grave. As the workmen gingerly lowered my mother's casket into the ground, I looked up and through the blurry crowd, desperately searching for one last chance. Then, through the numbness came a stabbing pain in my heart, as my focus sharpened and I realized that my father's loving eyes were staring into mine. For the first time in my life, I had his full attention and felt protected by him. In that instant, the painful past melted away and our future began. Although my mother was gone, my father had finally arrived—and I knew that it never would have been possible for both of my parents to be in my life at the same time.

By the time I was solidly into adulthood, thanks to the hard work and therapy, the anger I felt toward both my parents and had finally acknowledged, had already been slowly disappearing. As I stood at my mother's graveside—with my grief raw and my love immense—any remaining residue of anger just floated away, leaving in its place a sense of peace and hope within my broken heart.

Through the experiences I have shared, my understanding of my parents and of their life stories and points of view has deepened immeasurably. They always loved me and never intended to hurt me. Like you may have been, I was an innocent bystander who was sideswiped by my father's disease of alcoholism, and my mother taught me how to endure abuse past my breaking point rather than to get the hell out. Today, I am inspired by both of my parents. Mom used her experience to help millions of people around the world, and Dad is a powerful example of a transformation that is no small task to achieve, as well as a source of comfort and strength. I wish for you to have the fortunate experience that I have had.

In our final chapter, we will explore the transition from anger and hurt, to acceptance and healing.

---

### TAKEAWAY

#### How Unexpressed Anger Can Become Depression

There's no such thing as an alcoholic home where anger is not present. You walk in the door and you feel it. If you have grown up in this kind of a system, you are probably super-sensitive to it wherever you go.[6] —Dr. Jan

There was one family in my neighborhood that reminded me of my own. Whenever I went into their house, my stomach flip-flopped, and I felt anxious, just as when I was home. Those parents were always screaming at each other at the top of their lungs, calling one another degrading names. The kids seemed oblivious to it all and went about their business as if nothing was happening. Even when both parents weren't home at the same time and the house was quiet, you could cut the tension with a knife. Back then, it was comforting to know that another household was as tense as mine.

Today, this is not something that I can tolerate—physically or emotionally. Maybe you and I are alike in this, and you—like me—also find it difficult to be around people who are angry at one another and—like me—find it especially difficult to be around raised voices. Dr. Jan explained how different members of an alcoholic's family may express anger:

Usually with the alcoholic there is evidence of anger in terms of arguments, and yelling and screaming. There might be physical violence or storming out of the house, then generally the pattern is remorse and additional drinking and picking up the cycle again. This is part of what the child sees and what *their* anger is all about. There are a variety of responses in the case of the spouse. The first one is usually fear. They may also appear to be angry with the kids, and the kids will bear the brunt of all of this. The non-alcoholic spouse will also often become depressed—which is how they often internalize a large part of their own anger they cannot express because their fear of expressing it is so great.[7] —Dr. Jan

Dr. Jan said that children of alcoholics are often angry with the alcoholic, the codependent (non-alcoholic) parent, and with their siblings, but that often they do not express their own anger. She cautioned that when anger is not expressed, it can easily become depression.

Many ACoAs are what we call "chronically depressed." This means that there is an edge of sadness about them at all times. Many have said that they have been depressed as far back as they can remember. This is not unusual. It has to do in part with the anger that they have turned inward on themselves. It also has to do with the fact that they never had an opportunity to be children, and it also has to do with their experience of loss.[8] —Dr. Jan

About eight years ago, I went to see a therapist. It was a very difficult time in my life, and I was constantly on the edge of tears. Within ten minutes into my first session, she said, "We have to get you on medication. You're too depressed. I can't work with you like this." She said that once the medicine helped me feel better, we would be able to resolve the issues that had me so depressed in the first place. Then I could wean myself off the medication. I reluctantly agreed and started to take a low-dose antidepressant, which made me feel much worse. So she increased my dosage. And I became so much more depressed that I could barely get out of bed in the morning.

The medication was backfiring because, like many children of alcoholics, I have paradoxical responses to some medications, or sometimes need larger doses than normal for it to have an effect. I could see that, for me, this plan was not going to work. Besides, the reason for the depression was no mystery to me—I was full of rage at myself and my circumstances and felt powerless over them. I knew in my gut (and from what I had gleaned over the years from my mother's work) that my anger had to be acknowledged in a healthy, nondestructive way that would keep me sane and sober.

- Do you think that you are depressed? Have you felt this way for as long as you can remember?

- Thinking it through, do you believe that you might be turning your anger inward, and that this reaction might be causing you to feel this way?

- Do you think therapy and/or medication might help?

- Consider talking to your physician or therapist about how you are feeling. And consider what ways you can, as Dr. Jan suggests, let the anger leak out little by little, so it does not consume your life.

● ● ●

# CHAPTER 8

# Changing the Things We Can

One of the beautiful things about recovering as a family is that many times we start to talk to each other in ways that we have never talked to each other before. So family members begin to feel connected to one another, and that is absolutely wonderful. Even if the alcoholic doesn't become sober, the rest of the family can recover.[1] —Dr. Jan

When a family recovers together, it can become stable and loving. It can become the kind of family that we ACoAs never had, a family that positively influences current and future generations. Such a family has exhibited the courage to change the things they can. Making peace with the past helps us break the cycle of addictive behavior that became our unwelcome inheritance. The best way to heal the past is to build new, happier memories in the future, as we see ourselves as part of a colorful tapestry instead of a lonely, single thread. This is how we experience a paradigm shift. We discover that we are an important chapter in a larger story that began long before we were born and will continue long after we are gone. That realization can be both fascinating and empowering. It can also open the door to compassion and—in the best of all worlds—reconciliation with loved ones. Dr. Jan discusses the importance of changing the negative way we tend to think about ourselves and the enormous impact a positive view can have on our relationships with others:

> Empowerment is what it's really all about. What are the dis-empowering things we tell ourselves? "I can't do it. I'm not good enough. I shouldn't have to do it because I won't succeed." I find that a lot of folks do not have the vocabulary to change. But I say change that message to "I can, I am, I shall, I will" or "I may choose not to." If you change these messages, your relationships can change for the better. This is a challenge and an adjustment that may be uncomfortable in the beginning, but it is well worth the effort. The question is, and I worry about this: Can children of alcoholics relate to others on anything other than a level of pain? Do they wonder if they get done with their pain they'll have nothing to talk about?[2] —Dr. Jan

As I recounted earlier, my sweet friend Tommy often reminded me that "Feelings Aren't Facts." I recalled his wise words many times when I'd find myself slipping into the negative anger/blame cycle that could have ruined my relationship with my parents, other family members, or friends. As I matured and got the help I needed, I was able to eventually understand that my parents carried wounds from their childhoods—just as my grandparents no doubt bore their own scars. When I can recall my grandparents and parents, and their marriages and children, my view widens and patterns emerge. I can see that my mother and father had their own set of troubles that they tried to cope with. As parents, they did the best they could with what their parents gave them, just as I've done the best I could with what was given me. That may seem hard to believe, because it's so easy to judge our parents. But it is possible to change the way we view them. When we do this, we just might experience that old adage, "The older I got, the more I realized how much my parents have learned!"

As I've gone through the phases of my life so far, I have walked in my mom's shoes. She was a devoted mother, daughter, sister, and wife—a hardworking woman who took her power back in order to shoot for the moon. I now understand how she became the person she was meant to be. I even understand why she eventually gave me that car I used to steal from her! What a special, sweet, brilliant, loving, unique woman she was. I miss her every day.

I have also walked in my father's shoes and now understand the weight of the responsibility he had in providing for his family and the high level of stress he had in his work, despite what a talented journalist he was. I relate to the progression of his addiction—hitting rock bottom and living in recovery. But most of all, I understand and appreciate his transformation because I have a wonderful father today, and in him I now have a powerful role model for me and my children. Today I confide in him and seek his advice. How far we have come.

Now, as I look back to my own youth and young adulthood, I can also walk in my children's shoes. As I continue in my recovery and gain ongoing perspective on my life, I can see the ways in which their childhoods were similar to mine in ways that I did not intend. It still amazes me how I (and we) continued a pattern of addictive behavior and codependency during my children's growing-up years, even though I was not using drugs or alcohol during that time. I thought that being a substance-free and loving mother who never missed a gymnastics meet or a baseball game was enough to break the cycle of addictive behavior that was passed down to me. It never occurred to me that I continued to live crisis to crisis as though I were powerless over circumstances the way I was in my home as a child. As Mom said, I "came by it honestly"—"it" of course being that shadow that children of alcoholics are all too familiar with.

My unwelcome inheritance was not my fault, but it *is* my responsibility to be a catalyst for change in the family I have created. Today I can acknowledge my children's experience way deep down in my heart and apologize for not always being the mother they needed me to be, knowing how much it meant to me when my father acknowledged what I had been through as a child and he apologized to me. Today I continue to make living amends by being the mother they need me to be. Regardless of age, children need a healthy parent figure. That's another incentive for ACoAs to try to do better and to be better. It's never too late.

What about your family's story? How did addiction scar your parents? When you get to a point in your life and recovery that you are able to move beyond your immediate pain, I encourage you to try to stand in the shoes of each person in your family and attempt to see the world from their perspectives. Try to consider each individual's point of view with curiosity and without judgment. Try to imagine what they saw and experienced and felt when addiction invaded their homes. Try to appreciate their strengths and talents and specialness. Then try to open your heart to consider what it must be like for an alcoholic to live with what he or she did in the past and to know that it may have hurt their children. What is it like for you to live with the knowledge that your children may need healing as well?

If you are in recovery from an addiction yourself, think about how it feels when a loved one refuses to see the dramatic changes you have made in yourself. What does it feel like not to be forgiven when you are no longer the same person that hurt others in the past? Is it enough to make living amends and to apologize? Mahatma Gandhi is often quoted as saying, "Be the change you want to see in the world." What he actually said was even wiser: "If we could change ourselves, the tendencies in the world would also change. As a man changes his own nature, so does the attitude of the world change towards him. . . . We need not wait to see what others do." How can we extend that philosophy to respect, recognize, and embrace the changes in others that they have worked so hard to achieve?

As I discovered, some of our most traumatic childhood memories are of things that our alcoholic parent may not even remember. The toll alcoholism takes on bodies and brains can be long lasting. I suppose that's why it took years after Dad stopped drinking for him to really change his "dry-drunk" behaviors. And it took me a long time to be able to comprehend how sad Dad was when he finally saw how his behavior hurt our lives. I remember how confused he'd look when we'd tell him a story of a hurtful incident that he couldn't recall. I hope that you do not have to learn the hard way, as Mom did, that we can help our loved ones find their bottom and their recovery sooner by leaving the evidence of their behavior for them to see. Sometimes we think we are helping another person when we are really enabling them.

> When I am dealing with someone from an alcoholic home, I will say to the spouse, "When he busts up the furniture and passes out on the floor, don't clean up after him. Don't tuck him into bed. Let him wake up and find himself on the floor in his own vomit." If you clean up their messes, alcoholics who are prone to blackouts often won't believe what you say they did; they won't remember it. They need you to get out of the way. Most of us have a basic need or instinct to nurture, but sometimes we should do just the opposite.[3] —Dr. Jan

How sad for us ACoAs who have paid the price for our parent's disease by being brought up in the chaos of addiction, and how sad for alcoholics whose children won't forgive them despite the depth of remorse and the transformation these parents have worked so hard to achieve in order to be better parents. Even if it is a little late, is it ever too late? In my opinion, if there hasn't been a funeral, it's not too late.

With time—and with recovery—we hopefully begin to see our parents as people with their own stories and with their own struggles. Maybe we think our parents were terrible, but now we can see that, although that may have been true, their parenting may still have been an improvement over what their parents gave them. The baton is passed on to us, and, together, we ACoAs can commit to improving ourselves in order to do a better job of raising the next generation. Hopefully, we can begin to replace our anger and resentment toward our parents with compassion and perhaps even admiration of their survival skills. Perhaps we will be able to relate to our parents more than ever when looking at them through this new lens. When this happens, anger can fade away, making room for positive feelings—the same positive feelings that we want our own children to have toward us.

It's sometimes said that the opposite of fear is faith. As we ACoAs grow stronger in our recovery and build confidence in ourselves as individuals and as parents, our faith that the future can be different can deepen, which can help us get past the fear of trusting again. Mom explained why the willingness to go through this phase of rebuilding lives and relationships is so important.

> ACoAs must be able to trust that the person they care about will not want to hurt them and must be able to be honest about what they feel. This is the beginning of getting to know

someone in a very real way. Trust means allowing yourself to be vulnerable. But for ACoAs, vulnerability often meant they would probably get hurt. Allowing ourselves to be vulnerable also means that we can be open to love. For ACoAs, it also means they may be able to experience things that they have missed out on earlier in their lives. It does imply risk, and it is frightening, but the rewards can be life changing. If things don't turn out the way you hope, try to believe it will be okay. Your past has taught you that you can handle disappointment.[4] —*Dr. Jan*

Sometimes, however, trust is irreparably destroyed and reconciliation is not possible or not in our best interest. Maybe you are simply not ready to forgive or reconcile now. A therapist once said to me, "You don't really want to get better." I thought, "Why the hell do you think I'm here?" I *did* want to feel better, but I just wasn't ready to take certain steps at that time. If you do not feel ready, or if you feel that you are at risk of being emotionally or physically abused, heed those "red flags" and trust your instincts. Take care of yourself and keep your distance. Wait. Respect what your gut instinct is telling you.

When Mom and I had our heart-to-heart talks about accepting the past and moving forward, she acknowledged that there were circumstances where a relationship could be damaging to continue because the sickness is too great.

At times, the pathology that went on is far more serious than we were aware of, and I don't minimize that and I think we really need to recognize that possibility. We have to keep in mind that sometimes we have layers and layers of stuff here that may surface when we begin to take a look at it.[5] —*Dr. Jan*

In situations where reconciliation is not possible or inadvisable, there are times when we need to work through a relationship without interacting with the other person. My sponsor has suggested to me that praying for those people may help. At first I was very resistant to this suggestion, and I refused to wish anything good to come to someone who has made my life difficult. It was a struggle to find the motivation to wish good things for that other person—to see another point of view. Now I can pray for that other person to be healthy and happy for the sake of their families and others who love them and need them. I can even thank them for helping me grow and become a wiser and stronger person. Mom said it well:

> You can detach from those people that are toxic for you without denying the fact that they have influenced your life.[6]
> —Dr. Jan

As ACoAs learn the hard way, and as has been emphasized throughout this book, alcoholism is a family disease. Look through your family tree in any direction, and you can see how it has made its way through the branches of your family tree to you. You can see how it has affected the life you have lived and the way you have raised or are raising your children. As the saying goes, "Hurt People Hurt People," and ACoAs have the wounds to prove it. I may have been born into a legacy of beauty and brilliance, but I was also born into a legacy of addiction, and I am committed to doing whatever I can to protect my children and their children from experiencing what I did. I feel strongly that it's up to me to be a bridge toward healing for my family in all directions, no matter how frightening or uncomfortable this unchartered journey can be. I am ready to do what Mom urged ACoAs to do:

> Let's celebrate life. Let's celebrate life now and in the future with full awareness of the past and the depth it affords us to appreciate all that life can hold. That depth can enrich our lives in each day and in each moment. We can appreciate it now

and become comfortable with ourselves and that which stirs within us in the here and in the now.[7] —Dr. Jan

———————————————— TAKEAWAY ————————————————

### A Few Final Words from Dr. Jan

Much of the pain suffered by your family is reversible. Not only that but with your help, your children can be stronger and have great self-esteem because of their experiences. Yes, I mean that. Negatives can be turned into positives. It is all in knowing how. It has been my experience in counseling families that when I can enlist their help, improvement can be immediate and dramatic. You are a significant person in your child's life and in your family, and you can be a strong force for their well-being. There are many things you can do that will enhance a sense of self-worth in your children and improve your life in the process:

1. Continue to work on yourself and your own personal growth. Be the kind of person you want your children to imitate.

2. Listen to your loved ones and accept their point of view without interruption or judgment.

3. Tell the truth. Confronting reality is what brings us back to health.

4. Educate yourself, your children, and even your parents and other loved ones about the disease of alcoholism and encourage them to attend AA, Al-Anon, or Alateen.

5. Express your love, appreciation, and affection to others.

Ironically enough, the terrible illness that has hit your family can be used against itself. You suffered as a family divided by alcoholism, but you can recover as a family united because of alcoholism. Because of alcoholism, you became aware of yourself and your need to be a fully functioning family. Take advantage of that. Your children can be stronger because they have dealt with reality. They will most likely be less vulnerable because they have experienced the pain and faced it. We grow from the challenges in our lives. We grow more from the hard times, not the easy ones. As a family, you can become more fulfilled than if you were never forced to face yourselves. Helping your children build their self-esteem will help you build yours. And building your self-esteem will help your children. With recovery, the spiral can go upward throughout our families and into every area of our lives. Slowly but surely, the pattern can reverse itself with you in the driver's seat—because YOU ARE WORTH IT![8] —*Dr. Jan*

* * *

# Epilogue

Just shy of my fiftieth birthday, I look at a photograph of my childhood home. A wave of anxiety flushes my cheeks, and my insides instantly fill with the familiar dread that has colored my life. Just as the entire neighborhood knew our "secrets" back then, you know them now. If what they say in Twelve Step circles is true—that we are only as sick as our secrets and that the disease of addiction thrives in the darkness—then we ACoAs just might be able to interrupt the cycle of addiction by letting in the light. Our stories may be different, but the pain we ACoAs experienced as a result of addiction in our families is similar, and those old familiar feelings can serve as useful reminders of how far we have come. I am happy to report that today I can finally say with enthusiasm, "Life is good!"

My mother taught me that "if we have a unique perspective that can be of help to others, we have an obligation to tell our stories." When her colleagues and mentors insisted that children of alcoholics would outgrow their childhood trauma, she responded, "No, they won't grow out of it, they'll grow up *with* it!"

I have shared my experience and thoughts with you as so many of you have shared yours with me, because I feel that my mother would want me to follow the promptings of my heart and do so. We never know when something we say or a story we tell may help or give hope to another person and remind us that we are not alone. It has been a joy and honor to walk the path of recovery with so many ACoAs. I thank them all for the inspiration they have given me throughout the years and for keeping my mother's memory alive in such a meaningful way.

Buddha is believed to have said, "Our biggest mistake is that we think we have time." If these words ring true to you, I say, "Don't postpone joy."

• • •

# Notes

## Introduction

1. Janet Woititz, unpublished manuscript, 1986.

2. Janet Woititz (lecture on Adult Children of Alcoholics, Toronto, Canada, 1990).

3. Janet Woititz, "The Family as a Healthy System" (lecture, location unknown, 1982).

## CHAPTER 1: A Childhood from Hell

1. Janet Woititz, personal lecture notes, approximately 1985.

2. Janet Woititz, *Adult Children of Alcoholics,* expanded ed. (Deerfield Beach, FL: Health Communications, Inc., 1990), 77–78.

3. Janet Woititz, lecture notes, undated.

## CHAPTER 2: Unwelcome Inheritance

1. Janet Woititz, "Clinical Intervention—Making the Difference" (lecture, Princeton, NJ, 1985).

2. National Institute on Drug Abuse, "Drugs, Brains, and Behavior: The Science of Addiction," page last updated July 2014, www .drugabuse.gov/publications/drugs-brains-behavior-science-addiction/drug-abuse-addiction.

3. Paraphrased from American Psychiatric Association, *Diagnostic and Statistical Manual of Mental Disorders,* 5th ed. (Arlington, VA: American Psychiatric Association, 2013).

4. Janet Woititz, "Victims of Alcoholism" (lecture, location unknown, October 16, 1978).

5. American Society of Addiction Medicine, "ASAM Releases New Definition of Addiction," news release, August 15, 2011, www.asam .org/docs/pressreleases/asam-definition-of-addiction-2011-08-15 .pdf?sfvrsn=6.

6. Ibid.

7. *Merriam-Webster OnLine,* s.v. "brain," www.merriam-webster .com/dictionary/brain.

8. *Merriam-Webster OnLine,* s.v. "disease," www.merriam-webster .com/dictionary/disease.

9. Janet Woititz, "Adult Children of Alcoholics" (lecture, location unknown, 1985).

10. Janet Woititz, *Adult Children of Alcoholics,* expanded ed. (Deerfield Beach, FL: Health Communications, Inc., 1990), 183.

11. Ibid., xxvi–xxvii.

12. Janet Woititz, "Clinical Intervention—Making the Difference" (lecture, Princeton, NJ, 1985).

13. Melody Beattie, *Codependent No More: How to Stop Controlling Others and Start Caring for Yourself,* 2nd ed. (Center City, MN: Hazelden, 1992), 34.

14. Abraham J. Twerski, *Addictive Thinking: Understanding Self-Deception,* 2nd ed. (Center City, MN: Hazelden, 1997), 21–22.

15. Janet Woititz, National Association for Alcoholism and Drug Abuse Counselors (NAADAC) Conference, Atlanta, GA, June 12–14, 1985.

16. Janet Woititz (lecture on Adult Children of Alcoholics, Toronto, Canada, 1990).

17. Janet Woititz, Second Annual Conference on Family Issues in Chemical Dependency, location unknown, 1986.

18. Janet Woititz, "Clinical Intervention—Making the Difference" (lecture, Princeton, NJ, 1985).

## CHAPTER 3: A Look at Three Generations

1. Janet Woititz, personal notes, undated.

2. Ibid.

3. Janet Woititz, personal lecture notes, approximately 1985.

4. Janet Woititz, personal notes, undated.

5. Ibid.

6. Ibid.

**CHAPTER 4: Adult Children as Parents**

1. Janet Woititz, Second Annual Conference on Family Issues in Chemical Dependency, location unknown, 1986.

2. Janet Woititz, "The Family as a Healthy System" (lecture, location unknown, 1982).

3. Janet Woititz, "Adult Children of Alcoholics" (lecture, location unknown, 1985).

4. Janet Woititz, Second Annual Conference on Family Issues in Chemical Dependency, location unknown, 1986.

5. Janet Woititz, typewritten school paper, undated.

6. Janet Woititz, "Victims of Alcoholism" (lecture, location unknown, October 16, 1978).

7. Janet Woititz, "Clinical Intervention—Making the Difference" (lecture, Princeton, NJ, 1985).

8. Janet Woititz, "Adult Children of Alcoholics" (lecture, location unknown, 1985).

9. Janet Woititz, "Self-Esteem in Children of Alcoholics" (research paper, 1978).

10. Janet Woititz, "Clinical Intervention—Making the Difference" (lecture, Princeton, NJ, 1985).

11. Janet Woititz (lecture on Adult Children of Alcoholics, Toronto, Canada, 1990).

12. Janet Woititz, personal notes, undated.

13. Ibid.

14. Janet Woititz, "Clinical Intervention—Making the Difference" (lecture, Princeton, NJ, 1985).

15. Ibid.

16. Janet Woititz, personal notes, undated.

**CHAPTER 5: Adult Children Raising Alcoholics**

1. Janet Woititz, personal notes, undated.

2. Ibid.

3. National Council on Alcoholism and Drug Dependence, "Alcohol and Drug Information," http://ncadd.org/index.php/for-the-media/alcohol-a-drug-information.

4. Janet Woititz, "Building Self Esteem—Guidelines for Parents" (personal notes, undated).

5. Janet Woititz, "Victims of Alcoholism" (lecture, location unknown, October 16, 1978).

6. Janet Woititz, "Clinical Intervention—Making the Difference," (lecture, Princeton, NJ, 1985).

7. Janet Woititz, "Victims of Alcoholism" (lecture, location unknown, October 16, 1978).

8. Janet Woititz, "Building Self Esteem—Guidelines for Parents" (personal notes, undated).

9. Janet Woititz, "Victims of Alcoholism" (lecture, location unknown, October 16, 1978).

10. Janet Woititz, personal notes, undated.

11. Janet Woititz, first Adult Children of Alcoholics group meeting, 1981.

12. Timothy J. Healy (CASAC, Senior Addiction Counselor, St. John's Riverside Hospital, The New Focus Center, Yonkers, NY) in personal letter to Lisa Woititz, August 2014.

13. Professor V. G. Kay (past president, National Council on Alcoholism and Drug Dependence, NJ) in personal interview with Lisa Woititz, September 2014.

**CHAPTER 6: Breaking the Cycle**

1. Janet Woititz, "Bridging the Gap" (lecture, location unknown, 1988).

2. Janet Woititz, personal conversation with Lisa Woititz, undated.

3. Janet Woititz, first Adult Children of Alcoholics group meeting, 1981.

4. Janet Woititz, "Clinical Intervention—Making the Difference," (lecture, Princeton, NJ, 1985).

5. Janet Woititz, lecture notes, undated.

6. Ibid.

7. Ibid.

8. Janet Woititz, first Adult Children of Alcoholics group meeting, 1981.

9. Janet Woititz, personal notes, undated.

10. Janet Woititz, "Clinical Intervention—Making the Difference," (lecture, Princeton, NJ, 1985).

**CHAPTER 7: Breaking the Cycle of Anger and Resentment**

1. Janet Woititz, "Clinical Intervention—Making the Difference," (lecture, Princeton, NJ, 1985).

2. Janet Woititz, "The Family as a Healthy System" (lecture, location unknown, 1982).

3. Janet Woititz, "Healthy Families" (lecture, location unknown, 1988).

4. Ibid.

5. Ibid.

6. Janet Woititz, personal notes, undated.

7. Ibid.

8. Ibid.

**CHAPTER 8: Changing the Things We Can**

1. Janet Woititz, "Bridging the Gap" (lecture, location unknown, 1988).

2. Janet Woititz (lecture on Adult Children of Alcoholics, Toronto, Canada, 1990).

3. Janet Woititz, "Victims of Alcoholism" (lecture, location unknown, October 16, 1978).

4. Janet Woititz, personal notes, undated.

5. Janet Woititz, lecture notes, undated.

6. Ibid.

7. Janet Woititz (lecture on Adult Children of Alcoholics, Toronto, Canada, 1990).

8. Janet Woititz, personal notes, undated.

# About the Authors

From her preteen through adult years, **Lisa Woititz** worked closely with her mother, Dr. Janet Geringer Woititz, at Dr. Woititz's Institute for Counseling and Training, and took over managerial responsibilities at the institute after her mother's death in 1994. She has worked in the mental health, substance abuse, and criminal justice fields all of her professional life. She is a trained substance abuse counselor and crisis counselor, and she has served as a volunteer for NAMI (National Alliance on Mental Illness) for the families of persons suffering with mental illness. As a probation officer and peace officer, she supervised youth at high risk of incarceration, many of whom were the children of alcoholics, and conducted presentence investigations on adult criminal matters for the local courts.

Currently, Ms. Woititz serves as a liaison to the New York State Division of Disability Determinations facilitating mental health evaluations for claimants, many of whom have been affected by substance abuse and/or mental health issues. She is also a youth care worker for a homeless youth shelter in the Adirondack Mountains of upstate New York. She has recently been appointed to serve as a board member and secretary for the Town of Queensbury Ethics Board in Queensbury, New York. Most important, though, she is the mother of three amazing children.

**Janet Geringer Woititz, Ed.D.,** was affectionately known as "Dr. Jan" and "the mother of the Adult Children of Alcoholics (ACoA) movement." She was a therapist and president of the Institute for Counseling and Training in West Caldwell, New Jersey, which she founded to serve ACoAs and their families. Dr. Jan was an internationally recognized speaker, author, and trainer. She was the bestselling author of *Adult Children of Alcoholics* (1983), *Struggle for Intimacy* (1990), *Healthy Parenting* (1992), *Marriage on the Rocks* (1986), *Self-Sabotage Syndrome* (1987), *Home Away From Home* (1987), *Healing Your Sexual Self* (1989), *Lifeskills for Adult Children* (1990), *Lifeskills for Adult Children Workbook* (1991), *Going Home: A Re-Entry Guide for the Newly Sober* (1985), and *Guidelines for Support Groups: Adult Children of Alcoholics and Others Who Identify* (1986).

## About Hazelden Publishing

As part of the Hazelden Betty Ford Foundation, Hazelden Publishing offers both cutting-edge educational resources and inspirational books. Our print and digital works help guide individuals in treatment and recovery, and their loved ones. Professionals who work to prevent and treat addiction also turn to Hazelden Publishing for evidence-based curricula, digital content solutions, and videos for use in schools, treatment programs, correctional programs, and electronic health records systems. We also offer training for implementation of our curricula.

Through published and digital works, Hazelden Publishing extends the reach of healing and hope to individuals, families, and communities affected by addiction and related issues.

For more information about Hazelden publications,
please call **800-328-9000**
or visit us online at **hazelden.org/bookstore**.

# Other titles that may interest you:

## Adult Children of Alcoholics
Janet Geringer Woititz, Ed.D.
Written for adults who were raised as children in dysfunctional families, *Adult Children of Alcoholics* details the thirteen most common characteristics of adult children, provides an excellent guide for personal growth, and suggests topics for recovery group discussion. Published by Health Communications, Inc., and available through Hazelden Publishing.
Order No. 5001 (softcover)

## Recovering My Kid
*Parenting Young Adults in Treatment and Beyond*
Joseph Lee, M.D.
National expert Dr. Joseph Lee explains the nature of youth addiction and treatment and how families can create a safe and supportive environment for their loved ones during treatment and throughout their recovery.
Order No. 4693 (softcover), EB4693 (e-book)

## Days of Healing, Days of Joy
*Daily Meditations for Adult Children*
Earnie Larsen and Carol Larsen Hegarty
A year's worth of quotations, meditations, and closing thoughts encourage the small but consistent efforts of those seeking to give voice to the often timid, unsure, and frightened child within.
Order No. 5024 (softcover), EB5024 (e-book)